GOD LOVES YOU AND THERE'S NOTHING YOU CAN DO ABOUT IT

May you always know God's great love!

David Mann

GOD LOVES YOU

and there's nothing you can do about it

Saying Yes to the Holy Spirit

DAVID MANGAN

SERVANT
BOOKS

PUBLISHED BY ST. ANTHONY MESSENGER PRESS
CINCINNATI, OHIO

Cover and book design by Mark Sullivan
Cover images ©www.istockphoto.com/Stefan Klein/Neven Mendril

LIBRARY OF CONGRESS CATALOGING-IN-PUBLICATION DATA
Mangan, David, 1944-
God loves you and there's nothing you can do about it : saying yes to the Holy Spirit / David Mangan.
p. cm.
Includes bibliographical references and index.
ISBN 978-0-86716-839-6 (pbk. : alk. paper) 1. Holy Spirit. 2. Spiritual life—Christianity. 3. Christian life. I. Title.
BT121.3.M25 2008
248.4—dc22
2008001797

Published by Servant Books, an imprint of St. Anthony Messenger Press
28 W. Liberty St.
Cincinnati, OH 45202
www.ServantBooks.org

Printed in the United States of America.
Printed on acid-free paper.

08 09 10 11 12 5 4 3 2 1

To my wife, Barbara,
who has always been
my honest critic,
my greatest support,
my inspiration,
my strong right arm.

CONTENTS

ACKNOWLEDGMENTS

I would like to give great thanks to Bob Magill, who pushed and prodded me to do this writing. Without this impetus it probably never would have happened. I also owe a great debt to Marsha Williamson and Cindy Cavnar, whose kind encouragement kept me going and believing this was worth doing. A special thank you to my daughter, Aimee Bacik, whose early readings of this text were a great help.

God Is Amazing!

I REMEMBER THE SCENE AS IF IT HAD HAPPENED YESTERDAY. I was a junior in high school, sitting in English class listening to a debate. I don't remember the topic, but whatever it was I interpreted it as a significant Christian issue. As I listened I kept thinking, "Talk, talk, talk; it doesn't change anything. The truth is still the truth. I don't care what they decide about this. I stand for Christ!"

I had been raised in a good family and had thus far always tried to follow the Lord. I had thought that everyone was pretty much like me, since most of my acquaintances were. But it was dawning on me that having a faith life made me different—sometimes very different.

This was strictly a private moment. I didn't announce my findings to anyone. Yet announcing this fact to myself made a big difference in my heart.

By the grace of God I decided to embrace that difference. The way I saw it, God had given me everything and had asked me to give him myself in return. I wanted to learn what that meant and live it out. Not to live for Christ seemed foolish.

God is absolutely amazing. We deserve nothing, and yet he gives us everything. We turn our backs on him, and he still reaches out to us. When we were yet sinning, the Father sent Jesus, his only Son, to die for us, to save us and to bring us into a relationship with him (see Romans 5:6–11). And as if that were not enough, he gave us the Holy Spirit so that we could live out that relationship with his power.

And yet we still fall, question, doubt and give up sometimes. Have you ever felt that living the Christian life can seem like drudgery and endless labor—like trying to push a car uphill? Haven't you ever wished the Christian life were a lot easier? I know I have. I want God to endow me with some special ability so that I always know the right thing to do and have the power to actually do it.

If you're hoping that I have some magic formula for you, I'm afraid you're going to be disappointed. I've never discovered a magic formula for anything. But I do have good news: Although the Christian life on this side of heaven will never be problem-free, there is power to be had for living it out. That car you're pushing uphill has an engine and fuel, and you have the key.

What is the key that I speak of? It's God's amazing love for us. The key is that God walks with us in this life, and not as an observer but as a loving friend who carries us in our times of greatest need and who imparts his power to us even in our weakness. Knowing this and being able to tap into this love is nothing less than spiritual dynamite.

Do you need this spiritual dynamite? You bet your life you do! As we discover and acknowledge God's love, a whole new life opens up for us. Through that love we can discover how to appropriate his power to live the Christian life in an effective and grace-filled way.

Does that sound too simple? It's true. His love for us is so deep and wide that we can spend a lifetime discovering it. As we do, we will see remarkable things.

I want to share with you the truth of God's love and some of the ways he has chosen to impart it to us, his servants, his children, his friends. I pray that as you read this book, the Holy Spirit will move within you in a life-changing way. For when he acts, there is no limit to what can happen.

The best part is this: The Holy Spirit is more eager to act on our behalf than we are to have him do it. As you proceed, I invite you to pray with me, "Come, Holy Spirit!"

CHAPTER ONE

Good News

AS WE TRY TO FOLLOW GOD, WE OFTEN FIND TWO OPPOSING VIEWS fighting within us. The first view acknowledges the truth of Jesus' words, "You did not choose me, but I chose you" (John 15:16). "Wow," we think, "Jesus actually chose me—me!"

When I was a boy, we would form teams for baseball by choosing two players to be captains and having the rest of us line up and wait to be picked for one of the teams. The worst possible thing that could happen was to be chosen last. That meant nobody really wanted you on his team. You felt like a loser.

The greatest honor, however, was to be chosen first. This Scripture tells us that not only does Jesus want us on his team but also he picked us first, that is, before we picked him! He really wants us.

Now, even though I know this is the truth, I still hear the voice of the second view from time to time. You know the voice I mean. It's the one that says you don't deserve his love; you'll never measure up; everyone else can receive it but not you. It says, "Yeah, but if you only knew me…"

Sometimes I fall into this trap. I think that God could never choose me, let alone choose me first. The problem lies not in knowing the truth of God's love but in getting that truth from my head to my heart.

Let us consider this dilemma. Some have said that the distance of eighteen inches from the head to the heart is the longest journey in the universe. We cannot make that journey by sheer grit and determination. It takes God's grace along with our cooperation.

I remember quite vividly an incident in this journey that occurred when I was wrestling with a big issue in my life. I was in the midst of an especially difficult time, and I felt that I had failed the Lord miserably. I began to fear that Jesus was going to cut me loose. I was wondering how many times you can fail before he gives up on you.

My response to all of this was noble but futile: I determined not to make any more mistakes as I proceeded to dig out of my difficulties—as if that were possible. I didn't do this consciously, but in effect that is what I was doing. I was tense and worried about every decision as I tried to figure out God's will for me. I was more concerned about circumstances and actions than I was about loving God, and I slipped into regarding the Lord as an unreasonable taskmaster. The Christian life was becoming miserable.

Fortunately, God loved me enough to intervene. As I was praying one day, I was drawn to the Scripture passage Hosea 14:3–4: "'We will say no more, 'Our God,' to the work of our hands. In you the orphan finds mercy.' I will heal their faithlessness; I will love them freely, for my anger has turned from them."

I had read passages like this before, but this time was different. In Hebrews 4:12 it says that the Word of God is living and active. That was my experience in reading these verses. It was as though the words leapt from the page into my heart. In an instant I knew that I was making circumstances more important than God himself. I already knew this intellectually, but now my heart became involved, and I began to change.

Then the Lord spoke to me, not in an audible voice but in the quiet of my heart. He said, "David, you don't have to get it right this time either." As I considered this, all of the pressure I had been feeling began to disappear. I knew that God loved me whether I was right or wrong. His love for me was unconditional; it did not depend on my performance. I had learned all of this many times before, but now I *knew* it!

I think we often make the mistake of thinking that God is just like us. I'm sure glad he isn't. If we decided who received God's love and who didn't, the kingdom of God would be mighty small.

I don't presume to think that I know how much God loves me. His love is unfathomable and deeper than I will ever know, but there is a level of it that I do know, and it drives me to know more. His love is absolutely amazing!

We need to not expect God to act like us. We need a change of perspective. We need God's perspective, and we can only get it from him. I believe it was Abraham Lincoln who said that his greatest concern was not having God on his side but rather making sure that he was on God's side. What a great point of view!

When I think about a change in perspective, I remember a story about a monk who loved to smoke cigars. He was transferred to a new monastery, and when he arrived he asked the abbot if he could smoke while he prayed. The wise abbot said that he didn't think that was a good idea.

When the newly arrived monk went to the chapel to pray, he couldn't help but notice one of the other monks smoking a rather fine cigar. He went over to him and said that he had asked the abbot if he could smoke while he prayed, but the abbot had said no. The other monk replied, "You asked the wrong question. I asked him if I could pray while I smoked." Changing our point of view can make all the difference.

JESUS WANTS YOU!

I once heard someone say that Jesus didn't come to take sides; he came to take over. I think we need to let him do just that, especially in viewing things and living from his perspective. To refuse to live according to God's point of view is like waking up every morning, shooting yourself in the foot and then wondering why you walk with a limp.

The cornerstone of God's point of view is his love for us. Let us consider a little of what Scripture has to say about God's love.

First and foremost: God likes you. I mean, he really likes you! (I use the word *like* here because we have watered down the word *love* so much in our society that it has lost a lot of its meaning.)

Mark 3:13 says, "Jesus went up on a mountainside and called to him those he wanted, and they came to him" (*NIV*). I was meditating on this passage one day, and I got stuck on the fact that Jesus called "those he wanted." I realized that I had always assumed that Jesus called me because he had to, not because he wanted to. After all, it was his job. He is the Savior, and that's what saviors do.

I was so struck by this realization that I looked up the Greek word for *wanted* to see if it really had that element of personal desire in it—and it did! I was overwhelmed by how much Jesus actually wanted me to be around him. The King, the Master, the Creator wants *me*. Wow!

And it doesn't end there. In Micah 7:18 we read, "Who is a God like you, pardoning iniquity / and passing over transgression / for the remnant of his inheritance? / He does not retain his anger for ever / because he delights in mercy." It is noteworthy that this passage not only says that God will forgive us but that he delights in doing so. This is good news!

I can remember trying to manipulate my parents into giving me something. Occasionally, but not often, it actually worked. They would grant my wish begrudgingly just to get me to stop pestering them. My own children have done this with me a few times with some success.

God, however, does not give us his grace grudgingly. He doesn't show it through gritted teeth. He delights to show us mercy; he actually enjoys doing that. Sometimes his mercy doesn't come wrapped in the package we desire, but it is his mercy nonetheless.

God's great love and generosity are clear in Ephesians 2:4–5: "But God, who is rich in mercy, out of the great love with which he loved us, even when we were dead through our trespasses, made us alive together with Christ (by grace you have been saved)." He gave us his grace while we were dead in sin, that is, while we were still sinning. Isn't that amazing?

Have you ever tried to clean yourself up so you would look good to God? What a colossal waste of time! We can't clean up our act without him. The good news is that God loves you and wants to work through you just the way you are. He wants you *as is*! You don't have to change a thing to get him to love you.

Don't get me wrong here. I'm not saying that you don't have to change. My point is that changing your life is not the basis for God's loving you and being able to change you. In fact, his love for you and his presence in your life are the only things that can help you to change.

FAITH: HOW MUCH IS ENOUGH?

There are a group of incidents recorded in the New Testament that I like to call the "O you of little faith" Scriptures. These stories show the disciples having a problem exercising their faith. In each of these situations, Jesus "yells" at them, using the phrase "O you of little faith."

For example, in Matthew 8:26 we read, "He replied, 'You of little faith, why are you so afraid?' Then he got up and rebuked the winds and the waves, and it was completely calm" (*NIV*). And in Luke 12:28 Jesus says, "If that is how God clothes the grass of the field, which is here today, and tomorrow is thrown into the fire, how much more will he clothe you, O you of little faith!" (*NIV*).

In these two examples we find a thread that runs through all these stories. Jesus rebukes his followers for their small amount of faith, but he still delivers the goods: He gives them what they need. He doesn't tell them to come back when they have more faith. He supplies the need in the given situation.

If you feel that your faith is very weak and small, you qualify as a Christian. A little faith is enough; in fact, it's more than enough. All we have to do is use what faith we have.

The story of Peter's walking on the water gives us a great picture of Jesus' mercy in view of our lack of faith:

> "Lord, if it's you," Peter replied, "tell me to come to you on the water."
>
> "Come," he said.
>
> Then Peter got down out of the boat, walked on the water and came toward Jesus. But when he saw the wind, he was afraid and, beginning to sink, cried out, "Lord, save me!"

Immediately Jesus reached out his hand and caught him. "You of little faith," he said, "why did you doubt?" (Matthew 14:28–31, *NIV*)

You would think that if you were able to walk on water, even for a little while, you wouldn't doubt Jesus' word at all. But Peter did, and we probably do, too. When Peter cries for help, does Jesus say, "Sorry, Pete, not enough faith here. Come back when you have more"? Of course not! Jesus saves Peter in the very midst of his doubting. It is only after he has Peter securely in his grasp that he corrects him.

This is a great picture of how Jesus cares for us as well. Even in the midst of our doubts, he will come to us and help us.

I often have thought of what things were like in that boat after Peter climbed back in. He must have been wet, and he probably looked a bit haggard. Perhaps one of the other disciples teased him: "Hey, Pete, looking a bit wet there, aren't you?" But then Peter could have looked that disciple straight in the eye and said, "I may be wet, and I may have failed, but I also walked on water. Where were you?"

Even our half-finished attempts to serve God are great sources of grace. Reaching out to Jesus on any level is never a failure. He always reaches back.

In spite of knowing this, it continues to amaze me how easy it is to slip back into a mentality that says, "You need to pay your own freight; nothing in this life is free." I need to remember that the love I am offered in the shed blood of Jesus Christ is wider than I can ever imagine. Is it wide enough for you? You bet your life it is! And that is a bet you're going to win.

ANSWERING THE CHALLENGE

When I was beginning to try to live out my faith in a more radical way, I heard a story about the great evangelist D.L. Moody. The story goes that Moody was in a meeting where he heard someone say that the world had not yet seen what one person totally dedicated to Jesus Christ can do. Moody decided to accept the challenge to be that person. He went on to have a very powerful ministry of preaching and teaching.

When I heard this story, I knew that a long line of saints, stretching through the ages, had also demonstrated that kind of dedication. I decided that I wanted to be another one of those people.

As I look back on my Christian walk since then, I see an interesting mix of success and failure. I was hoping to go "from one degree of glory to another," as Saint Paul says in 2 Corinthians 3:18. The road turned out to be not as smooth as I had expected; sometimes it seemed downright impassable. I had imagined myself going from mountaintop to mountaintop, but I forgot to take the valleys into account.

Yet God carried me through it all. In fact, many of the times when I was most effective in serving God were when I was in the midst of a valley crying out for his mercy.

Now as I look back, I ask the D.L. Moody question a little differently. Has the world yet seen what one man can do for the kingdom of God—one man who is fully dedicated to Jesus Christ but who also is weak, prone to repeating dumb mistakes, losing his hair, gaining weight around the middle, not always hearing God very well and tempted to give up sometimes? I sense that God is asking me to be *that* man, because the result will be no different than it was for the earlier challenge I mentioned. The success of our attempts flows not from our efforts or grand notions but rather from the inexhaustible mercy of God.

O Lord, may I be that man!

CHAPTER TWO

Spiritual Dynamite

TO BE GOD'S MAN OR WOMAN, TO LIVE A LIFE FULLY DEDICATED TO him, we must live by his grace. We must avail ourselves of his tremendous power. I would like to share with you how he brought me into an experience of this power.

I wish I could tell you that I was a man of great faith whom God rewarded mightily, but that is not the case. I was just a weak but sincere Catholic who was frustrated with his inability to live the Christian life with the success that others seemed to experience. I was trying hard but just limping along.

The fact is that I was probably like most of you: normal. Isn't that good news? We can easily fall into the trap of thinking that God reveals his power only to the great saints in our midst, but God is eager to help us and provide for our needs even when we are weak and failing. We just need to turn to him and ask.

For me the experience began with trying to respond to the Second Vatican Council's call to the laity to be involved in the mission of the Church. I was eager to serve God in the Church, and I began to avail myself of any opportunity that was given to me. I was teaching religious education to eighth graders and serving as a lector and commentator, among other things. As I was trying to serve in these ways, I began to experience some of the weaknesses I mentioned earlier: doubts, fears, sin even.

In the religious education class, I came to a lesson on the Holy Spirit. I had to admit that I knew very little about the Third Person of the Blessed Trinity, at least from experience. About all

I knew was contained in a few pages of the *Baltimore Catechism* that I had dutifully learned in grade school. Since I didn't know much, I felt I couldn't teach the lesson well, and so I skipped it. I felt that integrity demanded that I not teach what I didn't know.

Around the same time I was invited to attend a retreat given through the chaplain's office of Duquesne University, the theme of which was the Holy Spirit. Duquesne University is a Catholic university in Pittsburgh, Pennsylvania, operated by the Holy Ghost Fathers. I had recently graduated from there, having been active in a student group called the Chi Rho Society. This organization sponsored activities to support students who were trying to effectively live out their faith. Now the Chi Rho Society was putting on this retreat, and the leaders asked me to give one of the talks.

I decided to attend the retreat, but I begged off on giving a talk. As I said before, I could not teach what I did not know. My goal for the retreat was a modest one: I would learn about the Holy Spirit and then teach the lesson to my class. Little did I know that God had much more in mind for me.

THE BIRTH OF A RENEWAL

Before I give any more particulars about my experience on this retreat, I think it would be helpful to share some background information. Events that took place on the Chi Rho retreat are often heralded as the beginning of the Catholic charismatic renewal. In this context the retreat is often referred to as the "Duquesne Weekend."

It is important to state that this book is not aimed at recruiting members for the Catholic charismatic renewal, although it would be a good thing if that happened. The goal, rather, is to help *you* receive the power of the Holy Spirit in your life, that he might stir up and renew in *you* the grace of the sacrament of baptism.

People involved in the charismatic renewal will tell you that its main goal is to help bring the grace of the release of the power of the Holy Spirit into the heart of the Church. A good illustration of this is found in a letter that Bishop Sam Jacobs of Louisiana wrote about the movement:

> On February 18, 1967, a group of college retreatants from Duquesne University, Pittsburgh, Pennsylvania, experienced the fulfillment of a promise of God in a mighty way. God in His great love poured out His Spirit in a new grace moment. He brought [the retreatants] into both the awareness and the power of the Baptism of the Holy Spirit. What they had experienced in the Sacraments of Baptism and Confirmation became more alive and real in them.[1]

In truth, the foundations of what happened on this retreat were laid long before 1967. Indeed, the roots of this experience go all the way back to the first Pentecost, when men and women experienced the power of the Holy Spirit in visible and audible ways (see Acts 2). Through the ages other holy men and women have cried out to God for more of his Holy Spirit.

Pope Leo XIII, at the urging of Blessed Elena Guerra, dedicated the twentieth century to the Holy Spirit. He opened the century by singing the hymn *Veni, Creator Spiritus*, "Come, Creator Spirit." Shortly after he uttered this prayer, stirrings began on several fronts of what is now called the charismatic renewal.

If we go back only a few years before the Duquesne Weekend to the Second Vatican Council, we can find foundations there, too.

For example, in the *Decree on the Apostolate of Lay People*, we read, "This most sacred Council, then, earnestly entreats in the Lord that all laymen give a glad, generous, and prompt response to the voice of Christ, who is giving them an especially urgent invitation at this moment, and to the impulse of the Holy Spirit" (*Apostolicam Actuositatem*, 33).[2]

What happened at this retreat was certainly not the first time something like this occurred, and it would not be the last. But it was an event that God used in a significant way for his purposes.

A friend used to say that if there was going to be an explosion of the Holy Spirit he just wanted to be close so that the power of God would touch him too. I suppose that's what happened to me. The Lord decided to bestow an amazing gift of love, and I was standing nearby. I don't think I can adequately express how privileged I was to be there and how much I didn't deserve it.

Something I learned from my experience on that weekend retreat is that it pays to stand close to God, even with less than pure motives. You get a lot of good things with very little effort, and sometimes you get credit for things that you had nothing to do with. We can see a good illustration of this principle in an interesting rule in baseball. If a batted ball hits a runner on base, he is declared out. The fielder who happens to be standing nearest to him gets credit for putting him out—even though he didn't do anything.

I feel like that fielder: I was in a place where God chose to act through the Holy Spirit in a significant way. I didn't know what was coming, and I certainly didn't deserve anything. Like a lot of us, I just wanted (and needed) more of God. I had not achieved any great heights of holiness, nor did I have any special knowledge. I received a lot more than I bargained for, and it was all God's doing.

SOMETHING MISSING

In preparation for the retreat, we were asked to read two things: the first four chapters of the Acts of the Apostles and a book called *The Cross and the Switchblade* by David Wilkerson. I dutifully read them, but most of the content went right over my head. The one thing I took from the readings was from David Wilkerson's book. He seemed to believe that God talked to him and told him what to do, and that if he obeyed, amazing things would happen. This belief intrigued me, and I wanted to find out more.

We started the weekend with what I would call a typical Friday evening on a retreat. We had a meditation, but I didn't give it much of my attention. I just wanted to get away from everyone and find some rest after a long week of work. The one thing that did catch my attention is that we began the evening, and every session thereafter, by chanting the hymn "Come, Holy Ghost."

The next morning after breakfast, we had the first major talk of the retreat. It was on the Acts of the Apostles, chapter one. This was the talk I had been asked to give, and not giving it turned out to be one of the best decisions I have ever made. A friend of mine was the presenter, and he did an excellent job.

More importantly, the Lord used one of the things the speaker shared to change my life completely. In Acts 1:8 Jesus says, "But you shall receive power when the Holy Spirit has come upon you." The speaker shared that the Greek word that is translated "power" in this passage is from the same root word from which we get the word *dynamite*. This hit me like a ton of bricks.

I knew that of the many words I could use to describe my spiritual life, *dynamite* was certainly not one of them. Although I loved Jesus and wanted to serve him, my experience of the spiritual life was primarily one of hard work. The Christian life certainly does involve hard work, but my friend's sharing showed me that there was a level of power that was missing in my life. I had experienced occasional bursts of that power—but more like a firecracker than dynamite. I didn't have an ongoing sense of God's love and power.

The more I considered what the Scripture had to say on the matter, the more I realized that there was something missing in my life. I knew that I wanted what was missing: I wanted this dynamite!

After the talk we broke up into small groups for discussion. I was anxious to share. The first thing I asked was, "Where's the dynamite?"

By education and career I am a mathematician, and I tend to begin my approach to any issue with reasoned logic. My argument was this: I received the sacrament of baptism, and when you're baptized you receive the Holy Spirit. So where was the dynamite? I received the sacrament of confirmation, and when you're confirmed you receive the Holy Spirit. Where was the dynamite? If I had received the Holy Spirit in these sacraments, why wasn't I experiencing his power in my life?

I wasn't being belligerent or challenging; I just needed to know.

Some of the participants on the weekend were going through a crisis of faith, questioning and challenging everything. In contrast, it never occurred to me to have a crisis over my questions. By God's grace I knew that the problem was not with God, with his word or with the Church. The problem was with me.

I figured that when I received these sacraments, God knew what he was doing. I also believed that the priest and the bishop knew what they were doing in administering these sacraments to me. But, especially when I was confirmed, I wasn't so sure that I knew what I was doing.

I was in sixth grade when I received the sacrament of confirmation—eleven years old. I learned all the information and was able to answer all the questions when I was quizzed on matters of faith. However, when the actual time of confirmation came, I was more interested in whether I was going to have a party and what gifts (unfortunately, not spiritual gifts) I was going to get than in any type of spiritual empowerment.

Now I shared with my small group that I knew the sacraments always give grace, but I also knew that they need to be received with faith. I wouldn't go so far as to say that I didn't exercise any faith at the time of my confirmation. I did believe, but my faith was fairly weak and very immature. I knew that I still had some responding to do regarding my baptism and confirmation.

Of course, I knew that this is always the case: We need to respond daily to what God has given to us through these wonderful sacraments. But I felt that there was something different going on here. The discussion in our group didn't resolve anything, but I left with a burning desire to pursue the matter.

GETTING READY

After we chanted "Come, Holy Ghost" again, we had the second presentation. This one was on Acts chapter two (I'm sure you can spot the progression here). I was very disappointed in this presentation. I had been looking forward to engaging the topic of spiritual power intellectually and learning what I was missing. I wanted to grapple with the issue. Since I was in a room full of college-types, I assumed some of the others were expecting the same. What happened was quite different.

The main focus of Acts chapter two is what happened on the Day of Pentecost. Our speaker that day didn't present any arguments or try to convince us of anything. Her presentation was brief: She read the chapter and made a few comments. Then she said, "This still happens today."

I was stunned. I wrote in my notebook, "I want to hear someone speak in tongues—ME!" I'm not sure why, but then I wrote, "Be a fool for the Lord." I didn't realize it at the time, but I was about to do both.

I didn't have a clue as to what this all meant. I really wanted the speaker's words to be true, and I knew that if it happened to someone else I would probably doubt it. I was hungry for more, and I was determined to keep beating on God's doors until one of them opened. I still have my notebook from that weekend, and I periodically like to read those notes and appreciate what God has done for me then and since. It continues to stir my faith.

We returned to our small groups for discussion. Interestingly enough, I quickly forgot about what I had just written about the gift of tongues and returned to the issue of "Where's the dynamite?" I didn't connect the two ideas at all, but I was sure that this "dynamite" was something that God wanted me to pursue.

As we continued talking I began to ask myself how we could respond to what seemed to be God's initiative. I have never seen myself as a creative type or an idea person, but I came up with an idea that I thought was pretty good.

Most of us had been baptized as infants. The Church provides opportunities to renew our baptism—during the Easter liturgy, for example—so that we can make this sacrament our own. Could we also do this for confirmation? I thought we could ask the chaplain on the retreat to devise some sort of prayer so that those who desired it could pray for the renewal of their confirmation.

When I suggested this, one of the retreat leaders who was in our small group asked me very pointedly, "David, if you do this, are you ready for what God will do?" That put a little fear in me. I responded, "No, I'm not ready, but I want to do it anyway."

I figured that if you always waited till you were ready to do something, you wouldn't end up doing very much. I assumed that God wouldn't give me anything I couldn't handle, and that he would take good care of me even in my ignorance. Our discussion time ended, but I finally felt that I was getting somewhere.

All of the retreat participants reconvened so that each small group could share the fruits of their discussion. When it was our group's turn to share, the representative included in our report the idea about renewing our confirmation. The whole group considered the possibility of making this prayer but then rejected it. The way I read the tone of the response was that the others thought our group was taking things a bit too seriously.

I was very disappointed. It seemed that my one good idea was being swept aside. I was still determined but not quite sure how I should handle all of this. The session ended, and we broke for lunch.

After lunch I took a walk on the retreat grounds with a friend of mine, Patti Mansfield, who was in my small group. As we walked we shared our disappointment with the way the idea about renewing our confirmation had been received. We both felt that it would be a good way to respond, and we couldn't understand why the group as a whole wasn't interested in the proposal.

As we were about to reenter the retreat facility, I turned to Patti and said, "Even if no one else is going to renew their confirmation, I am!" Patti said she felt the same way.

CALLING ON GOD

When we went into the building, we were greeted with some disturbing news. The facility we were using was in the country, and the only source of water was a natural spring. The pump that brought the water from the spring into the retreat house had broken. A repairman had been called, but he was not able to come until Monday (this was Saturday afternoon). We would have no water for drinking, cooking or bathroom facilities. It looked as if the retreat would have to end.

I remember thinking to myself, "This can't be; I'm just beginning to get some answers to the questions about my spiritual life."

The leader who shared this information with us then said, "Why don't we go to the chapel and pray?" For some reason I found this suggestion a little frightening.

Don't get me wrong: I was accustomed to praying. I just don't think I had ever been faced with a situation in which I needed an immediate answer to my prayer. I had prayed for the conversion of Russia, but I was in no hurry. I had prayed for the starving in India, but since I never saw them, I could afford to be patient. (Of course, these were examples more of immaturity than of patience.)

Our situation now was something else. I felt strongly that ending this retreat would be a mistake. God was doing something with us, and I was finally doing business with him. We had to continue.

I then realized why I was afraid. What if God said no? Could I handle that? What would it do to my faith?

Even so, I was eager to go and pray. Remember, the discussion group leader had asked me earlier if I was ready for what God would do, and I had said, "No, I'm not ready, but I want to do it anyway." It was now time to "put up or shut up." I went to the chapel in fear but also in excitement.

The chapel was a small room on the second floor. There were no chairs, only a carpeted floor with an altar, backed by a large window overlooking the woods outside. A tabernacle sat on the altar. We all knelt before the presence of the Lord and began to pray. I prayed in a couple of ways I never had before.

First I prayed out loud in my own words. Prior to this, praying out loud in a group was reserved for rote prayers and responses at Mass. In this case I needed to express myself more naturally. It felt great to pour out my heart to God. I knew he already knew how I felt, but it seemed very important for me to vocalize my concerns.

Then I did something that was most unusual for me. In a sudden burst of faith, I knew that God had answered our prayer, so I thanked him out loud for giving us the water we needed.

Have you ever said something and immediately wished you could grab the words and shove them back in your mouth, as though they had never been uttered? As soon as I had thanked God out loud, my great burst of faith was replaced by regret. I thought to myself, "What a foolish thing to say; how presumptuous!"

Yet I had said it, and part of me was still glad I had gotten it out there. My words seemed to end the prayer. After all, how can you keep on praying for something when some foolhardy soul just thanked God for already doing it?

We all left the chapel and went back downstairs. My faith didn't feel terribly strong, but I went immediately to the kitchen to see if we had water. If God uses the foolish and the helpless, why not me? I went right to the sink and turned on the faucet, and water came out—more strongly than it had before the problem! WOW! I was excited beyond words.

I went out into the foyer and told everyone there, "We have water, we have water!" The funny thing was that most of the retreatants had not known the water was gone. Only the few of us who came back from lunch early had been told about it. The rest of the retreatants were trying to figure out why I was so excited.

I found out a little later that while we were praying, the repairman had had a change of heart and had come and fixed the pump. But it didn't matter to me how God had answered the prayer, only that he had saved our retreat.

HERE'S THE DYNAMITE!

I decided to go back to the chapel to thank the Lord for answering my prayer. I figured that if you're going to moan and groan to Jesus, your thanks ought to be at least as loud. So up the stairs I went.

I had left the chapel only minutes before, and my experience of God's presence had been real but not unusual. Now I was about to experience him in an entirely new way. I never could have imagined that what was about to happen to me was even possible.

As I entered the room, I experienced the love and presence of God in a way that was so real to me that it was like walking into a physical object. I felt as if I was wading into the room rather than walking. In fact, it was like trying to walk while being completely submerged under water. I made my way toward the altar, and the next thing I knew I was prostrate on the floor before the Blessed Sacrament.

I'm not sure how much I was completely overcome by his presence and how much I cooperated with the experience. I had never seen anyone prostrate himself before, and it seemed a little strange to me. One thing was certain though: I was afraid, and the Lord's presence was so strong that it seemed that the only reasonable place to be was on my face, bowing before him.

I feared that I was going to explode. Something welling up within me drew me to worship. The "explosions" inside me kept coming and coming. After a while I worked myself up to a sitting position. In some fashion I beheld the Lord and worshipped him.

Then another strange thing happened. I opened my mouth to vocalize my worship and thanksgiving, and the words came out in a language I had never heard before. This really scared me. I stopped doing it, thinking, "That's weird!" Yet somehow I knew that this was good.

I remained quiet on the outside but exploding on the inside. I knew that the Lord was with me, caring for me and imparting his power. It felt like more than I could handle, yet at the same time I knew he wouldn't give me more than I could handle. It was then that I remembered my relentless question, "Where's the dynamite?" Here it was! Of course it had been there all along, but God chose that moment to light the fuse.

I remained in the chapel for a while—how long I'm not sure. It might have been one hour, or it might have been three. Any sense of the passage of time completely escaped me.

Eventually I got up to leave because I feared that I couldn't take this experience any longer. I felt as if my body might actually give out under the weight of God's awesome power. I made my way to the door and out into the hall.

As I went down the stairs, I held on to the railing because I was very unsteady; I thought I might fall down the stairs. When I reached the bottom step, all of a sudden I doubted everything. I remember thinking, "Mangan, you've flipped out. Get a hold of yourself. You're a mathematician; you're a logical man. Get a grip!"

Faced with my doubts, I did what any good scientist would do. I went back to the laboratory—in my case, the chapel. I had to talk this over with the Lord.

I reentered the chapel, and again I found myself before the Blessed Sacrament in profound worship. The power of God's presence seemed even stronger than before. How long I stayed this time was no easier to tell than before. Who could care how long it was!

I again hit the point when I felt that I had to leave. I didn't think I could handle the strong experience of God anymore. I got up and made my way down the stairs as before. When I hit the bottom step, the doubts came again.

Without hesitation I turned and made my way back to the chapel. When I entered the room, the deep experience of God happened all over again, perhaps even more powerfully. (I was handling it better each time.) I was soon absorbed in prayer and worship.

I was afraid to say anything out loud, thinking that it might come out again in words I didn't understand. Yet I knew that I had to say something to God. What I ended up doing was unlike me— and a little embarrassing. I "looked" at the Lord as best I could, dug deep down into my gut and yelled the loudest and wildest yell I could muster: "YAAAHOOOOO!"

My "rebel yell" was heard all over the retreat house. Many people thought that something awful had happened, so someone came running up to the chapel to check. He found me sitting before the tabernacle. When I turned and saw him, all I could say was, "It's so good. It's *so* good!"

The guy turned and left, still wondering if I was OK. I stayed there again for a while and then got up to leave. This time I made it past the bottom step. I began to realize that I didn't have to be in the chapel in order to experience the presence of God, although it seemed more intense there. God was with me, working with me in a special way.

BEYOND GOOD

At this point I wanted to talk to someone more experienced than I in spiritual matters, so I sought out the chaplain and one of the leaders of the retreat. As best I could, I laid out for them what had been happening to me. I then began peppering them with questions. Was this a valid experience? What does it mean? What does God want of me? What would the Church say?

The leaders were very helpful. They said that, of course, they couldn't be certain at this point, but it seemed like a valid experience. The Church has a long history of God's power touching his people. As far as what God might want of me, they said I would have to wait to hear from him on that score.

As I turned to leave, one of the leaders asked me an interesting question. He asked if at some time I had said anything in a strange language. I told him I had, but it had seemed kind of weird so I had stopped it. He pointed out that there is a spiritual gift in the New Testament called the gift of tongues, and that was probably what I had experienced. He suggested that I give it a chance if it happened again.

I left the room with a light heart filled with joy and a spring in my step. I headed back to the chapel. This was way past good!

I spent most of the remaining retreat time in the chapel enjoying the Lord's love and presence. The experiences weren't as intense as before, but they were just as rich.

I started to wonder if I was alone in this blessing. Then I noticed that some of the other retreatants were spending a lot of time in the chapel and had silly grins on their faces. The first one I noticed in this regard was Patti Mansfield, the friend who had joined me in wanting to renew her confirmation. Once when I was walking up the stairs for another visit in the chapel, she was coming down. I said, "You too?" She only responded, "Me too." I was glad that I was not alone.

Sunday morning came, and there was a presentation on Acts chapter three. I only remember the topic because it was next in the sequence. I sat in the back of the room because I was still experiencing the Lord's presence in a strong way, and I wanted to be inconspicuous.

My attempt at anonymity failed miserably. As the talk began I tried to listen, but I was lost in the presence of Christ. I was overcome by joy, and I remember thinking that I wanted to laugh out loud. Of course I wouldn't do that because I didn't want to disturb the others, but then I did it anyway. I was laughing so hard that I fell out of my chair. So much for being unobtrusive!

I realized that I was quite a distraction, so I got up, apologized and left the room. I found a private place and continued roaring with laughter for a long time. I felt as though I was being cleansed deep within.

The remainder of the retreat was a distant observation of what the others were doing and a continual walk in the presence of the Lord Jesus. I was lost in Christ, and there was no other place I wanted to be. I drove home from the retreat in excitement, somehow knowing that I was embarking on the greatest adventure of my life.

TAKING THE NEXT STEPS

For the next year I continued to walk in a wonderful sense of God's presence and amazing power. I knew that I was in a very special time, when the Lord was instilling deeply in me the call to be a radical disciple—to be like David of old, "a man after his own heart" (1 Samuel 13:14). The Lord seemed to be bringing me into spiritual realms that were way beyond my spiritual maturity. He planted deep within me a clear vision of what a "normal" Christian life was supposed to be like.

As I returned to a daily walk that was more on the level of my spiritual maturity (or lack thereof), I burned with the desire to be and do what the Lord had placed in my heart. At that point I had many questions. I still wondered if I was weird. I wondered what the Catholic Church thought about all of this. I wondered what people would think of me.

I have found some answers to my questions. Am I weird? I guess I no longer care about that very much; in fact, I think I'm the normal one. Am I alone? Hardly! The latest estimate I have heard is that over 150 million Catholics have had a similar significant experience of the power of the Holy Spirit in their lives. Among all Christians the number is more like 450 million.

As far as what the Catholic Church has to say, at least three popes have made it clear that they think the charismatic renewal is great for the Church (more about that later). What some members of other churches have had to say, however, has challenged me on several occasions. When I have been invited to share my story in Pentecostal churches, people have challenged me about being a Catholic. After all, this didn't seem like a typical Catholic experience. Sometimes people even asked me when I was going to leave the Catholic Church. I found out that in most cases the people asking this question had had similar experiences and, for various reasons, had left the Catholic Church.

Although I sympathized with the dilemma of those who were asking me this question, I had to tell them that I had found my experience of God in the Catholic Church, not in leaving it. I had wanted to live my life of faith more effectively, and I had been praying for a renewal of the sacraments of baptism and confirmation. Then God showed himself to me. I had to challenge my questioners, just as they challenged me, and let them know how I saw God working.

As for my wonderings about what other people think of me, I guess I still wonder about that, but I'm getting better at not caring so much about it. I want everyone to like me, but I want God's love a whole lot more. My heart burns to be radical for him. As long as I'm pleasing him, what anyone else thinks is of little value.

In considering any event of great importance, it is valuable to look at it from different points of view. In my telling of the story of the Duquesne weekend, I mentioned a good friend of mine, Patti Mansfield. Patti and her husband, Al, are still very active in the charismatic renewal. I conclude this chapter with Patti's account of the weekend in the hope of giving you a clearer picture of that tremendous event.

PATTI'S PERSPECTIVE

People frequently ask me if I ever get tired of telling the story of the Duquesne Weekend. I never do because it's a love story, the story of God's gracious and extraordinary response to the prayer of some very ordinary people.

In Luke 11 Jesus says, "Ask, and it will be given you; seek, and you will find; knock, and it will be opened to you…. If you then, who are evil, know how to give good gifts to your children, *how much more will the heavenly Father give the Holy Spirit to those who ask him!*" (Luke 11:9, 13, emphasis added). Here is an unfailing principle: From the first Pentecost on, the Holy Spirit has always come in response to fervent prayer—prayer that is hungry and thirsty for more of God, prayer that asks, seeks and knocks.

The entire twentieth century was dedicated to the Holy Spirit in a special way. Blessed Elena Guerra urged Pope Leo XIII to call the entire Church to pray more fervently to the Holy Spirit— to be, as it were, a permanent cenacle of prayer. In the prayer to the Spirit that we prayed for the Second Vatican Council, we asked with the same fervor: "Divine Spirit, renew Your wonders in this our day as by a new Pentecost."[3]

In the spring of 1966, two Duquesne University professors were asking, seeking and knocking. They had pledged themselves to pray daily for a greater outpouring of the Holy Spirit in their lives, using the beautiful Sequence Hymn of Pentecost. In the midst of this time of prayer, some friends gave them two books: *The Cross and the Switchblade* and *They Speak With Other Tongues*. Both books describe the experience of the baptism in the Holy Spirit. After reading these, the professors realized that this baptism in the Spirit was precisely what they were searching for.

In January 1967 some Catholics from Duquesne attended their first interdenominational charismatic prayer meeting, known as the Chapel Hill meeting, in the home of Miss Flo Dodge, a Spirit-filled Presbyterian. Interestingly enough, a few months before these Catholics came, the Lord had led Flo to read Isaiah 48, where he announces that he will do something new.

Indeed, God was about to do a new thing among Catholics as a result of the prayer meeting. The people from Duquesne were impressed with what they witnessed there. On January 20 two of the men went to a second meeting of the group, and they received the baptism in the Holy Spirit and began to manifest charismatic gifts. They returned home to pray with the two other people, who had not attended that night.

At this time I was a member of the Chi Rho Scripture study group that met on the Duquesne campus. The two professors who had received the baptism in the Holy Spirit served as moderators of Chi Rho, and although they did not tell us outright about their charismatic experience, those who knew them well noticed that they radiated a new joy. We were planning for a retreat in February, and the professors suggested a new theme: the Holy Spirit. In preparation for the retreat, they told us to pray expectantly and to read *The Cross and the Switchblade* and the first four chapters of the Acts of the Apostles.

A few days before the retreat, I knelt in my room and prayed, "Lord, I believe I've already received your Spirit in baptism and confirmation. But if it's possible for your Spirit to be more at work in my life than he's been up until now, *I want it!*" The dramatic answer to my prayer was soon to come.

On February 17 about twenty-five of us left for The Ark and the Dove Retreat House on the outskirts of the city. As we gathered for each session, our professors told us to sing as a prayer the ancient hymn "Veni Creator Spiritus," "Come, Creator Spirit."

On Friday night there was a meditation on Mary. Let me say that this was a very appropriate beginning. Cardinal Leo Jozef Suenens of Belgium would later write "that Jesus Christ continues to be born mystically 'of the Holy Spirit and of Mary' and that we should never separate what God has joined together."[3] Just as Mary was in the Upper Room at Pentecost, she is with us whenever we return to the Upper Room. She will teach us how to surrender to the Father's will; how to be faithful to Jesus, even to the cross; how to pray with a humble, pure and docile heart for more of the Holy Spirit; how to be one family. If we want to proclaim Jesus to the world, we need the Holy Spirit, and we need Mary, the Mother.

Then we had a penance service. In John's Gospel we read that when the Holy Spirit comes, he will convict the world of sin (see John 16:8). That's what happened among us as we repented in the sacrament of reconciliation.

On Saturday a member of the Chapel Hill prayer group came to speak on Acts chapter two. All we were told was that she was a Protestant friend of our professors. Although her presentation was very simple, it was filled with spiritual power. She spoke about surrendering to Jesus as Lord and Master. She described the Holy Spirit as a Person who empowered her daily, just as he had the apostles. Here was someone who really seemed to know Jesus intimately and personally! I knew I wanted what she had, and I wrote in my notes, "Jesus, be real for me."

In the discussion following the talk, David Mangan proposed that we close our retreat by renewing our confirmation: that we, as young adults, say our personal yes to the Holy Spirit. I linked my arm through his and said, "Even if no one else wants to do this, I do." Then I tore a sheet of paper out of my notebook, wrote, "I want a miracle!" and posted it on the bulletin board.

On Saturday night a birthday party was planned for a few of our members, but there was a listlessness in the group. I wandered into the upstairs chapel, not to pray but to tell any students there to come down to the party. When I entered I knelt in the presence of Jesus in the Blessed Sacrament, literally trembling with a sense of awe before his majesty. I knew in an overwhelming way that he is the King of Kings, the Lord of Lords.

I thought, "You had better get out of here quick, before something happens to you." But overriding my fear was a much greater desire to surrender myself unconditionally to God. I prayed, "Father, I give my life to you. Whatever you ask of me, I accept. If it means suffering, I accept that too. Just teach me to follow Jesus and to love as he loves."

In the next moment I found myself prostrate, flat on my face, and flooded with an experience of the merciful love of God, a love that is totally undeserved yet lavishly given. What Saint Paul writes in Romans 5:5 is true: "God's love has been poured into our hearts through the Holy Spirit." My shoes came off in the process—I was indeed on holy ground (see Exodus 3:5). I felt as if I wanted to die and be with God.

The prayer of Saint Augustine captures my experience: "You have made us for yourself, and our heart is restless until it rests in you."[4] As much as I wanted to bask in God's presence, I knew that if I, who am no one special, could experience the love of God in this way, anyone across the face of the earth could do so.

I ran down to tell our chaplain what had happened, and he said that David Mangan had been in the chapel before me and had encountered God's presence in the same way. Two girls told me that my face was glowing, and they wanted to know what had happened. I wasn't familiar enough with Scripture to know the passage in 2 Corinthians that describes Moses' shining face when he returned from the mountain. Saint Paul writes, "And we all, with unveiled face, beholding the glory of the Lord, are being changed into his likeness from one degree of glory to another" (2 Corinthians 3:18).

I led these two students into the chapel and began to pray, "Lord, whatever you just did for me, do for them!" That was probably the shortest Life in the Spirit Seminar on record!

Within the next hour God sovereignly drew many students into the chapel. Some were laughing, others crying. Some prayed in tongues; others (like me) felt a burning sensation coursing through their hands. One of the professors walked in and exclaimed, "What is the bishop going to say when he hears that all these kids have been baptized in the Holy Spirit?" The birthday party that night was the one God had planned in the Upper Room chapel. It was the birth of the Catholic charismatic renewal!

When we returned to campus, we created quite a stir. One friend told me, "Patti, if I didn't know you better, I would say you were drunk!" Like the apostles after Pentecost, we couldn't help but speak of the things we had seen and heard. We literally stumbled into charismatic gifts like prophecy, discernment of spirits and healing. One of our professors witnessed to his friends at Notre Dame and Michigan State University: "I no longer have to believe in Pentecost; I have seen it!"

Since 1967 the grace of this new Pentecost has spread from a handful of students on the Duquesne Weekend to 119 million Catholics around the world. Why? Certainly not because of our holiness or expertise. We were not founders, only witnesses to God's action. The grace of baptism in the Spirit has spread around the world because God is determined to send forth his Spirit to renew the face of the earth (see Psalm 104:30)!

CHAPTER THREE

Walking in the Power of the Holy Spirit: Why Not You?

YOU NOW HAVE TWO ACCOUNTS OF THE ACTION OF THE HOLY SPIRIT. It's important to realize that the Lord deals with each of us in a way that perfectly suits our needs. One of the symbols for the Holy Spirit in the Scriptures is oil (see 1 John 2:20, 27). Just like oil, the Holy Spirit takes the shape of the container into which he is poured. When we yield to his presence, we are completely new, and yet we remain ourselves.

After I had received the wonderful experience of renewal in the Holy Spirit, one of the things that concerned me was the question of how others could experience it too. Was this an isolated event that only happens occasionally, or was it common? I soon realized that this renewal was not common but that it could be.

SHARING THE BLESSING

One of the first things I did after I returned home from the retreat was to share what had happened to me with the woman who later became my mother-in-law. When she actually believed me, I asked her if she wanted me to pray for her to receive this gift, too. At this time I still had no knowledge of what to call this experience—other than "the dynamite."

When we prayed, she experienced the renewal. I was excited beyond words. This increased my boldness to share with others, and I soon discovered that God was more than eager to bring those who ask into this power of the Holy Spirit. (A couple months later I was privileged to pray over my future wife, a wonderful young woman named Barbara.)

The Lord was beginning to work all over the place. We began to see a spiritual explosion of God's power. Today there are hundreds of millions of people who participate on some level in this spiritual movement. Central to this renewal is the experience of the power of God that is often called the baptism in the Holy Spirit.

Let me note again, however, that participation in this movement—or any movement, for that matter—is not a prerequisite for receiving the wonderful blessing of the baptism in the Holy Spirit. I have had many occasions to share about my experience, and it isn't unusual for someone to approach me afterward and tell me of a similar experience that he or she had never understood. In fact, I have heard countless stories of people, unaware of any movement, crying out to Jesus in their need and receiving this experience. And the Lord has been pouring out this grace throughout the history of the Church.

This gives rise to some questions. What is the baptism in the Holy Spirit? What does it look like? What does the Catholic Church have to say about it? Why should I want it? Can you get to heaven without being baptized in the Holy Spirit?

I would like to answer the last question first, because it reveals a little of my approach to spiritual matters. Can you get to heaven without this experience? Yes, but why would you want to? If God is offering a grace, I want all that I can get. If God is giving, I'm taking—and I'm getting in line twice! It's not that I'm greedy; it's that I'm needy.

When I look at the New Testament and consider the Day of Pentecost and other events that demonstrate the outpouring of the Holy Spirit, I see holy men and women reaching out to receive more of God. I see the Blessed Mother, the apostles and other disciples going for it all. If these powerful, holy people needed this grace, then I need it all the more. In fact, who do I think I am if I say I don't need it?

I have seen thousands of normal folks like you and me reach out to God for this grace, and their lives have never been the same. They did not become problem-free all of a sudden, but they are in closer contact with the One who is the solution to all of their difficulties.

THE SPIRIT AND THE CHURCH

Next let us consider the questions "What is the baptism in the Holy Spirit?" and "What does the Catholic Church have to say about it?" I'll attempt to answer these questions rather informally, since there are already several works that do a great job of answering them theologically and sacramentally. Two that I highly recommend are *Fanning the Flame: What Does Baptism in the Spirit Have to Do with Christian Initiation?* by Fathers Killian McDonnell and George Montague (Liturgical, 1991). The other is *Sober Intoxication of the Spirit: Filled with the Fullness of God* by Father Raniero Cantalamessa, the preacher to the papal household (Servant, 2005).

When asking about the baptism in the Holy Spirit, the first and most important thing to say is that we are dealing with a scriptural phenomenon. The gift of the Holy Spirit is a work of God, not something people thought up. Consider these two examples from the book of Acts:

When the day of Pentecost had come, they were all together in one place. And suddenly a sound came from heaven like the rush of a mighty wind, and it filled all the house where they were sitting. And there appeared to them tongues as of fire, distributed and resting on each one of them. And they were all filled with the Holy Spirit and began to speak in other tongues, as the Spirit gave them utterance. (Acts 2:1–4)

While Peter was still saying this, the Holy Spirit fell on all who heard the word. And the believers from among the circumcised who came with Peter were amazed, because the gift of the Holy Spirit had been poured out even on the Gentiles. For they heard them speaking in tongues and extolling God. Then Peter declared, "Can any one forbid water for baptizing these people who have received the Holy Spirit just as we have?" (Acts 10:44–47)

Second, I think the simplest way to look at the baptism in the Spirit is as the stirring up of the grace already bestowed on us in the sacrament of baptism. Bishop Sam Jacobs of Louisiana wrote of those who received the baptism in the Spirit: "What they had experienced in the Sacraments of Baptism and Confirmation became more alive and real in them."[1]

When I received the baptism in the Holy Spirit, all I asked for was the renewal of my confirmation. I had never heard of the baptism in the Holy Spirit, but my Catholic faith told me that there was more to be had.

Bishop Jacobs went on to say, "It is clear…that this grace of Pentecost, known as Baptism in the Holy Spirit, does not belong to any particular movement but to the whole Church. In fact, it is really nothing new but has been part of God's design for His people from that first Pentecost in Jerusalem and throughout the history of the Church."[2]

In his book *Come, Creator Spirit*, Father Cantalamessa calls the baptism in the Spirit "a renewal and a reactivation and actualization, not only of baptism, but of all that Christian initiation involves."[3] He also says:

> Through what aptly has come to be called the baptism in the Spirit, we experience the Holy Spirit, the Spirit's anointing in our prayer, power in our apostolic service, consolation in our trials, light upon the choices we make. More basic than any manifestation of the Spirit in the charisms, this is the first way we perceive the Holy Spirit, as transforming us from within, giving us a desire to praise God and a taste for praise, leading us to discover a new joy in life, opening our mind to understand the Scripture, and above all teaching us to proclaim Jesus our "Lord."[4]

The experience of the baptism of the Holy Spirit is a stirring up of the grace that we received in baptism and confirmation, grace that was initially poured out on the first Christians on the Day of Pentecost. This renewal of our baptism and confirmation gives us a personal experience of the grace of that first Pentecost. Father Cantalamessa says, "The new Pentecost is…happening now…. Many seriously believe that this is the greatest spiritual upsurge in all the history of the Church: in a mere eighty years, from zero to about four hundred million people…. [W]e need to take note of what is called the baptism of, or in, the Holy Spirit, which is the special grace at the core of all this vast spiritual revival."[5]

Support for this renewal is coming from the most trustworthy voices in the Church. In 1975 Pope Paul VI welcomed to Rome the international Catholic charismatic renewal conference. In

May 2004, during vespers on the eve of Pentecost, Pope John Paul II said, "Thanks to the Charismatic Movement, a multitude of Christians, men and women, young people and adults have rediscovered Pentecost as a living reality in their daily lives. I hope that the *spirituality of Pentecost* will spread in the Church as a *renewed incentive to prayer, holiness, communion and proclamation.*"[6]

In a previous statement the pope already had expressed encouragement: "This was the unforgettable experience of the Second Vatican Ecumenical Council during which, under the guidance of the same Spirit, the Church rediscovered the charismatic dimension as one of her constitutive elements."[7]

As we consider these words, I believe we find that the baptism in the Holy Spirit is not some rare, unusual experience. This grace of the Holy Spirit is meant to be part of the normal experience of Christian life. It is for all members of the Church, from "the greatest" to "the smallest." After all, without the active power of the Holy Spirit, it is difficult—if not impossible—to live the full Christian life.

EXPERIENCING LIFE IN THE HOLY SPIRIT

The next question to answer is, what does the baptism of the Spirit look like?

There is no single answer to this question; a lot can be said about it. First let me say that the outward appearance is somewhat different for everyone. As I have already mentioned, the Holy Spirit takes the shape of the container he is poured into, just as oil does. When people are baptized in the Holy Spirit, some laugh, some cry, some feel great peace and some don't feel anything special at first but later realize new joy, new peace, new spiritual power.

Being baptized in the Holy Spirit is usually accompanied by the reception of spiritual gifts, especially the gift of tongues, and other gifts often follow. However, it is important to note that most of the work of the Holy Spirit is subtle and therefore hidden initially. We see it more as it grows within us. Saint John of the Cross said that the Lord often hides his greatest works from us lest we ruin them with pride.

There are many experiences of the Holy Spirit that easily go unnoticed. For example, when we receive any of the sacraments, we encounter Christ, and we receive the Holy Spirit. Sometimes we are blessed with an awareness of what has happened, and sometimes not, but God has come to us and changed us nonetheless. If we see the baptism in the Spirit as the awakening or stirring up of the grace of the sacrament of baptism, it's no wonder that it may work in a similar fashion to the sacrament of baptism.

Even though much of the work of the Holy Spirit is hidden from us, there is much that we do notice. We begin to know God's love and guidance more by experience. His teaching becomes more alive to us. The Bible has a deeper personal meaning.

And we can pray in a new way. In fact, the Holy Spirit often enables people to pray in a language that they don't know.

THE GIFT OF TONGUES

Have you ever had something in your heart that you could find no way to express adequately in words? I have found that the gift of tongues gives me the ability to vocally express to God things that are deep in my heart.

This gift of tongues is often the cause of questions and criticism as well. Some people, although they acknowledge that exercise of the gift is scriptural, are quick to call it the least of the gifts.

Whether that is the case I do not know—or care, for that matter— for the least of God's gifts are infinite in scope because they come from him.

In 1 Corinthians 14, Saint Paul says to follow the way of love and eagerly desire spiritual gifts, especially the gift of prophecy (verse 1). He then gives guidelines for the use of the gift of tongues. In addition he says that he would like everyone to speak in tongues but even more to prophesy (verse 5). If he gives guidelines for the use of the gift of tongues, he certainly must expect us to use it.

To me the gift of tongues sounds like a great starting place to being open to the Spirit. In fact, over the years my experience has been that this gift continually helps me to open up to the wider scope of what the Lord wants to do with me.

It's not that I haven't had some questions and doubts. After I had been praying in tongues for a little while, I began to wonder, is this real? Is it necessary? Am I crazy? As I would do with any difficulty, I asked Jesus to help me deal with these questions.

One Friday evening a short time after the Duquesne weekend, I attended a prayer meeting. After we had finished praying, a man who was new to our meeting approached me and asked if I would speak in tongues for him. I told him no, explaining that it was a gift of prayer and that I didn't feel comfortable giving him a "demonstration." I then mentioned that I would be glad to pray for him, and if I felt led to do so, I would pray in tongues. He accepted my offer, and I began to pray for him.

I have found that when I don't know what to pray for, the gift of tongues is especially helpful, so I prayed in tongues on that occasion. When I finished praying, the man told me why he wanted to hear this gift in operation. He was a linguist and was doing a study to determine if the gift of tongues was real. He told me that I had been praying in a form of French that is no longer spoken. It was an early form of the language and played a role in the development of modern French similar to the role of Middle English in the development of modern English.

The linguist was very excited. He felt that God had sent me to help him along on his journey. He didn't know that I felt that God had sent him to me, to help me out of my questions and doubts. Only a handful of people on earth could have recognized the language that I was speaking, and God sent one of them to me!

The linguist then asked me to pray for him some more. When I finished this time, he said, "Now you're praying in Arabic!" I guess Jesus was adding an exclamation point.

RECEIVING THE GIFT

I was at a conference when a nun who was an acquaintance came to me for prayer. She said that she had received the baptism in the Holy Spirit about three years before but had never received the gift of tongues. She was very disappointed and wondered if God was displeased with her.

Now, I do not subscribe to the view that the gift of tongues is *the* evidence that one is baptized in the Spirit. We receive the baptism in the Holy Spirit by faith, just as we do everything else in the Christian life. When we ask, we know that we have received because it is part of God's plan for us, and we believe him. The fact that we are unworthy of God's gifts only points to the fact that these are gifts—unmerited favors.

I let this sister know that, and I assured her that God was not displeased with her. In fact, I was fairly certain that he was very pleased with her. On the other hand, I told her that the Lord is generous with the gift of tongues. And when Saint Paul said that he wanted us all to speak in tongues, he meant it!

I asked this sister if she had ever prayed for the gift of tongues specifically, and she said that she had. I was confident then that her prayer had been answered. Her problem was not that she hadn't received the gift but that she didn't know how to use it.

Acts 2:4 says that the disciples were filled with the Holy Spirit on the day of Pentecost and began to speak in other tongues. The clear implication here is that the apostles began the speaking process. This sister's difficulty was that she was expecting God to take over her mouth and move it for her—in a sense, forcing her to speak in tongues. Although she was knowledgeable about the role of free will and the necessity of cooperating with God's grace, she didn't apply that knowledge in this case.

I shared with the sister that all she had to do was open her mouth, start praying and then choose to not pray in English (or any other language that she already knew). She looked at me as if I were crazy. She said that she didn't know how to do that.

I asked if she had ever tried making up her own language as a child. She said yes, and so I suggested that she try that again now and see what God would do. As I said this to her, I thought of Psalm 81:10, "Open your mouth wide, and I will fill it." Perhaps in this case he would fill her mouth with speech in tongues. Exercising great humility, she said she would try.

I suggested that we pray for the gift of tongues in the following way: As soon as we finished asking for it in English, we would continue praying out loud, but at that point, no English would be allowed. We prayed, and then the sister continued making sounds. It is important to note that as she did this, she felt no particular spiritual consolation. In fact, the main thing she felt was embarrassment. She said a few words and looked at me as if to say, "I did it; so what?"

What happened next amazes me to this day. The sister spoke what seemed to her to be a string of sounds, but in fact they were the words of a language. I recognized the language that she had spoken: It was Swahili! What is especially interesting is that I only knew a handful of words in Swahili, and those were the words she spoke. A friend who wanted to be an African missionary was studying the language, and he had taught me those few words.

Since I am a mathematician, I immediately thought about the odds of opening your mouth, forming random sounds and having those sounds be words in a language. Pretty slim odds, I would say. What are the odds of doing this when there is only one other person in the room and the words you form are in a language he knows? Slimmer still. What are the odds if he only knows a handful of words in that language, and those are the words you say? Astronomical! God did fill her mouth.

I shared all of this with her and asked her if she realized that she had prayed in tongues. She said, "I'm not sure," and I wasn't surprised. She couldn't let her spiritual life rest on my faith and knowledge. She needed to do business with God directly.

I told her that I was not going to try to convince her of the reality of what had just occurred. That was God's job, and he is a lot better at it than I am. Besides, I was leaving after the conference, and my assurance was not enough for her to build upon. We prayed again, and I asked the Lord Jesus to convince her of what he had just done. I only asked her to trust enough to spend a little time each day in praying this way in addition to her normal modes of prayer. She said she would.

When I saw this nun the next morning, she was positively aglow, so I asked her what had happened. She said that as she knelt at her bed the night before to say her prayers, she began to pray the way we agreed. She felt the Lord's presence in a powerful way and literally burst forth in tongues of praise. She had received the gift of tongues before, but as she began to exercise the gift, the Lord in his mercy also gave her the spiritual consolation and assurance she longed for.

OUT OF THE MOUTHS OF BABES

As I said before, the baptism in the Holy Spirit is truly a gift from God—an unmerited favor. Maturity isn't a prerequisite. Neither does being baptized in the Holy Spirit bring instant maturity; that takes time.

One question I asked myself when my children were young was, how soon do they need renewal in the Holy Spirit? When can they receive it?

When I was about to send my first child off to kindergarten, I was more than a little concerned for her spiritual well-being in an environment that I didn't trust. I wanted her to be spiritually equipped for the adventure, but I wondered how much a little five- or six-year-old could receive. I decided to find out.

I had often helped present a series of teachings called the Life in the Spirit Seminar. This series is designed to help participants learn about and receive the baptism in the Holy Spirit. I considered the material and tried to figure out how I would present it to a small child. I asked my daughter if she would be interested in doing this, and we made plans to give it a try.

A couple of my daughter's friends were also interested. With their parents' permission I launched the experiment. We had an overnight retreat at our house, and the result was that three six-year-olds were baptized in the Holy Spirit and received the gift of tongues.

The retreat worked so well that we started a family custom of doing something like this with each of our children when he or she reached five years of age. Some have questioned me as to whether this renewal in the Holy Spirit was real, but more than twenty-five years later, my children still experience the power of the Holy Spirit in their lives.

The most interesting development occurred when our fourth child, David, reached five years of age and was included in our renewal in the Spirit sessions. We prayed for him, and he was baptized in the Spirit and received the gift of tongues. We did not include his two-year-old sister, Ann, in our prayer session. We "knew" that she was too young. What happened the next day, however, changed our minds on that point.

After his morning kindergarten session, David was playing with Ann in the basement very quietly. Every parent knows that when children are quiet, you had better watch out, so my wife, Barbara, peeked into the area where they were playing. David was telling Ann, on his own level, about the love of Jesus, just as we had shared with him the evening before.

David asked Ann if she wanted more of Jesus in her life, and she said yes. He then led her in a simple prayer, asking Jesus to come into her life, and she responded. Then he asked her if she wanted the Holy Spirit. When she said yes, he led her again, and she said, "Jesus, give me the Holy Spirit." Then David said, "Now talk like this," and he began to pray in tongues. So did Ann.

When I came home Barbara told me what she had witnessed and asked me if I thought it was real. We figured then that it was, and after more than twenty years of seeing the power of the Holy Spirit in Ann's life, we know that it was real. Apparently Ann was not too young to have the grace of the sacrament of baptism stirred up in her.

If a five-year-old can pray for a two-year-old and bear fruit, I think it's safe to say that this is not rocket science. All we need is simple faith.

As I said before, the baptism in the Holy Spirit does not bring instant maturity and understanding. When my children received this blessing, they had a child's grasp of it. As they grew up, their faith and understanding had to grow, too. Our times of family renewal and prayer nurtured and sustained what had begun so early.

I'm fully convinced that the Lord wants to be just as generous with everyone who turns to him. Teaching and understanding about this are certainly important, but there is no substitute for simply asking.

TOP TEN REASONS TO BE BAPTIZED IN THE HOLY SPIRIT

I hope that what I have shared has whetted your appetite for experiencing the power of the Holy Spirit. I would like to share my "Top Ten" reasons for why you should want to be baptized in the Holy Spirit:

1. This gift comes from God, and we know that everything that he wants to give us is for our good. What better reason do we need?

   For John baptized with water, but before many days you shall be baptized with the Holy Spirit. (Acts 1:5)

   And Peter said to them, "Repent, and be baptized every one of you in the name of Jesus Christ for the forgiveness of your sins; and you shall receive the gift of the Holy Spirit. For the promise is to you and to your children and to all that are far off, every one whom the Lord our God calls to him." (Acts 2:38–39)

2. This is one of the things Jesus came to do.

> [John said,] "I baptize you with water for repentance, but he
> who is coming after me is mightier than I, whose sandals I am
> not worthy to carry; he will baptize you with the Holy Spirit
> and with fire." (Matthew 3:11)

> And John bore witness, "I saw the Spirit descend as a dove
> from heaven and remain on him. I myself did not know him;
> but he who sent me to baptize with water said to me, 'He on
> whom you see the Spirit descend and remain, this is he who
> baptizes with the Holy Spirit.'" (John 1:32–33)

3. You need to experience a relationship with all three members
   of the Holy Trinity. Knowing the Holy Spirit is just as important
   as knowing the Father and knowing Jesus.

> And when Jesus was baptized, he went up immediately from
> the water, and behold, the heavens were opened and he saw
> the Spirit of God descending like a dove, and alighting on him;
> and behold, a voice from heaven, saying, "This is my beloved
> Son, with whom I am well pleased." (Matthew 3:16–17)

> If the Spirit of him who raised Jesus from the dead dwells in
> you, he who raised Christ Jesus from the dead will give life to
> your mortal bodies also through his Spirit who dwells in you.
> (Romans 8:11)

4. With the power of the Holy Spirit, you will do the same things
   as Jesus—and even greater things! (Do you think you can do
   these on your own power?)

> Truly, truly, I say to you, he who believes in me will also do the works that I do; and greater works than these will he do, because I go to the Father. (John 14:12)

5. Baptism in the Spirit is part of the normal Christian life.

> While Apollos was at Corinth, Paul passed through the upper country and came to Ephesus. There he found some disciples. And he said to them, "Did you receive the Holy Spirit when you believed?" And they said, "No, we have never even heard that there is a Holy Spirit." And he said, "Into what then were you baptized?" They said, "Into John's baptism." And Paul said, "John baptized with the baptism of repentance, telling the people to believe in the one who was to come after him, that is, Jesus." On hearing this, they were baptized in the name of the Lord Jesus. And when Paul had laid his hands upon them, the Holy Spirit came on them; and they spoke with tongues and prophesied. (Acts 19:1–6)

6. You need power to witness for Jesus, and God gives you this power through the Holy Spirit.

> But you shall receive power when the Holy Spirit has come upon you; and you shall be my witnesses in Jerusalem and in all Judea and Samaria and to the end of the earth. (Acts 1:8)

7. God wants to give you spiritual gifts.

> To each is given the manifestation of the Spirit for the common good. To one is given through the Spirit the utterance of wisdom, and to another the utterance of knowledge according to the same Spirit, to another faith by the same Spirit, to another gifts of healing by the one Spirit, to another the work-

ing of miracles, to another prophecy, to another the ability to distinguish between spirits, to another various kinds of tongues, to another the interpretation of tongues. All these are inspired by one and the same Spirit, who apportions to each one individually as he wills. (1 Corinthians 12:7–11)

Having gifts that differ according to the grace given to us, let us use them: if prophecy, in proportion to our faith; if service, in our serving; he who teaches, in his teaching; he who exhorts, in his exhortation; he who contributes, in liberality; he who gives aid, with zeal; he who does acts of mercy, with cheerfulness. (Romans 12:6–8)

8. You are a Christian, and Christians live their lives by the power of the Holy Spirit.

But I say, walk by the Spirit, and do not gratify the desires of the flesh. (Galatians 5:16)

And those who belong to Christ Jesus have crucified the flesh with its passions and desires.

If we live by the Spirit, let us also walk by the Spirit. (Galatians 5:24–25)

9. We don't want to oppose God. If he wants to pour out his Holy Spirit, who are we to deny him?

As I began to speak, the Holy Spirit fell on them just as on us at the beginning. And I remembered the word of the Lord, how he said, "John baptized with water, but you shall be baptized with the Holy Spirit." If then God gave the same gift to them as he gave to us when we believed in the Lord Jesus Christ, who was I that I could withstand God? (Acts 11:15–17)

10. Baptism in the Spirit comes highly recommended from the most trustworthy sources, beginning with Jesus himself and continuing through Pope Benedict XVI. On the vigil of Pentecost 2006, the pope said, "Upon all of you I invoke an outpouring of the gifts of the Spirit, so that in our time too, we may have the experience of a renewed Pentecost. Amen!"[8]

The number of people who have received the baptism in the Holy Spirit numbers in the hundreds of millions. Why not you?

CHAPTER FOUR

How Do You Hear the Lord?

Have you ever been in a situation and wondered, "What does God want me to do?"

If it is simply a matter of deciding right versus wrong, we have a great deal of data for the decision—the Ten Commandments, Jesus' teaching and other Scripture, Church teaching and so on. But often the choice we face isn't one between right and wrong.

What if we want more than what is merely acceptable? What if we want God's best, the course of action that will build his kingdom, bless those we love and bring us as close to Christ as possible? There is good news: God is eager to communicate with us on these matters.

One of the principal tenets of being a Christian is obedience to God. With all of our hearts, we want to be willing, obedient servants. When faced with an important decision (or maybe even a fairly minor one), we ought to ask ourselves, "What does Jesus want me to do?"

We know that Jesus sent the Holy Spirit to communicate with us and to guide us, but often it doesn't seem very easy to figure out what he wants for us. Our anxiety is complicated by the fact that we hear some Christians speak as though they have a "hotline to heaven." They describe being in a situation where the Lord "told" them what to do or "led" them in a certain direction. Their stories often sound like, "Then he said...and I said...and he said...and so I did it, and it worked!"

Hearing this can make you feel as if you don't hear the Lord very often or very well or even at all! You might be so intimidated by this kind of talk that you back off on trying to "hear the Lord" yourself when you need his guidance.

But in the end that's no help, because we really do want to know what God has to say. So what do we normal folks do, those of us who don't seem to have a hotline to heaven?

This is a reasonable question that deserves a reasonable answer. I would like to share some of the significant ways in which I hear the Lord. I think that much of what I have to share will resonate in you, and you might even say, "I hear the Lord that way too," or, "You know, that's happened to me, but it never occurred to me that the Lord might be speaking to me." I believe the Lord shows up in the strangest places, and therefore we need to be open to any way he may try to communicate with us.

A READY AND WILLING SAVIOR

The first thing to say is that God *wants* to communicate with us. Consider two Scriptures that confirm this truth.

The first half of 2 Chronicles 16:9 says, "For the eyes of the LORD range throughout the earth to strengthen those whose hearts are fully committed to him" (*NIV*). This passage refutes a common attitude that makes us act as though hearing the Lord were a hide-and-seek game, and we're trying to catch God. Now, it might be a hide-and-seek game, but it's the other way around: God is trying to catch us. He is much more eager to speak to us and have us hear his voice than we are to hear it.

The verse says that God's eyes search throughout the earth looking for you, and that he does this in order to strengthen your heart. That's pretty amazing. The God of the whole universe is seeking you out to help you. You must be very important to him! Keep this in mind when you're seeking his will in a particular situation: He is very eager to communicate with you.

The second Scripture that tells us that God is eager to communicate with us is Hebrews 11:6: "And without faith it is impossible to please him. For whoever would draw near to God must believe that he exists and that he rewards those who seek him."

Some people say, "I prayed, but nothing happened. Maybe I should have prayed this way, or maybe I should have prayed that way." If you think like this, you will end up feeling like you're a rat in a maze, and nothing could be further from the truth. When we pray, God is always there; he always cares. We need to believe this in order to hear God.

Granted, we may not see or understand God's answer in a particular situation. Sometimes his wisdom is beyond us, or for some reason his answer is hidden from us. Sometimes it's better that we don't know what God is doing.

But very often God does want us to know, and we're afraid to ask and listen for his answer. Even though we might never admit this, we often pray with the following attitude: God is sitting on a throne, arms folded. He doesn't really want to do anything for us, but if we bug him enough, maybe he will. It's almost as if he is sitting there saying, "Impress me. Your theology had better be good, or you're getting nothing."

That is really *not* the true picture. God is not that hard to get along with. It is true that we want to have good theology, but that isn't a prerequisite for hearing the Lord. If it were, imperfect people like us would never have a chance.

The mental picture that I would like all of us to have is very different. Jesus is right on the edge of his throne, and he is ready to move as soon as we start to say his name. We want to say, "Jesus, come and help me." As soon as we say, "Je…," he is there! He is off the throne, on our laps and in our faces—right away. We don't always know that is what is going on, but he is really that eager.

I think that the Bible makes this clear. And having this attitude really helps us hear the Lord.

Let me say that I have never had an audible dialogue with God. When he and I are communicating, my voice is the only one I hear. I'm not saying that two-way audible dialogues can't happen, but they certainly aren't common. God truly speaks to us, but the reality of how he does it—or at least how we experience it—is usually quite different from an audible conversation.

When you really press someone who is describing a type of "He said, then I said" dialogue, he usually realizes that he is giving the wrong impression. The actual experience is more like "I had a desperate need, so I prayed. I think the Lord might have said something to me, but I wasn't sure. Was that the Lord? What does that mean?"

Then the person wrestles with the word he has received, perhaps for a long time, and he might not even do anything about it. The Lord comes back and nudges him again, and he wonders, "Is that the Lord, or is that me?" Maybe he goes to talk to somebody, saying, "I'm not sure if I really heard the Lord or not."

There could be days or even weeks of agony trying to figure out what the Lord is saying. When he finally does whatever he thinks the Lord is asking him to do, God blesses the situation in an amazing way. *Then* he really knows that the Lord was speaking all along. So when he tells the story, it becomes condensed into "Yeah, I was seeking the Lord, and he came to me and said to do this, and I did it, and it all worked out."

Sometimes you might hear the Lord right away and act on it. Occasionally I do. However, most of the time I kick and scream and try to figure things out, and then I think maybe I know what to do. The important thing to realize is that God does speak to us. Here's one example from my life.

AN ADVENTURE WITH GOD

Several years ago I was attending a graduate institute of theology at Marist College in Poughkeepsie, New York. After 11:00 AM Mass one Sunday, I remained afterward to pray. I wanted to offer my day to the Lord, so I prayed, "Lord, I'm free this afternoon. If there is anything you would like me to do, let me know."

Almost immediately the thought popped into my head, "Go see Harald." My friend Harald Bredesen was the pastor of a Dutch Reformed church in Mount Vernon, New York, about ninety miles south of Poughkeepsie. I thought that it would be nice to go and visit him, but I was wondering if this was actually what the Lord wanted me to do. I wrestled with the idea a bit and came to the conclusion that I wasn't really sure. So I weighed my choices and their consequences, and I decided to go see Harald, thinking that maybe the thought was from God.

Besides, I had nothing to lose. The worst that would happen was that I would see an old friend. As you can see, this adventure was not beginning with a great act of faith.

I arrived at the church and found Harald among a crowd of people in the middle of a potluck dinner in the congregation hall. When he saw me he called out over the crowd, "David, do want to be on television?" If you knew Harald you would not find this greeting unusual.

After exchanging pleasantries, Harald explained that a friend of his was looking for a Catholic to interview on his TV program. This friend had heard about Catholics who were experiencing the power of the Holy Spirit in their lives. Since I'm always eager to share about how powerful and active God is among Catholics, I gladly said that I would do it.

It was then that Harald said that the TV station was in Norfolk, Virginia, and I had to get there quickly, since the show was that very day. Harald had recruited another person for the show, so the two of us headed out together to La Guardia Airport.

We had a significant problem, however. This was the Sunday of the July 4th weekend. Norfolk, Virginia, has a large naval base, and it seemed as if its entire population was trying to get back to Norfolk that day. We went to the Delta Airlines counter, and the best we could do was become numbers seven and eight on the standby list.

We decided to take a chance that we would get on and made reservations for the return flight. We then went to a coffee shop to wait and pray. Our prayer was simple: "Lord, if you want us to do this, please get us there." We returned to the boarding area and, lo and behold, we became the last two standby passengers to get seats on that flight.

While we were in the air, a flight attendant told us that the plane would first stop in Newport News, Rhode Island, and we might get bumped off the flight at that point. We prayed again, and when we landed in Newport News, about as many people got off as on, so we kept our seats. Finally we made it to Norfolk. We were surprised to find a limousine waiting to take us to the TV station in nearby Portsmouth.

When we arrived at the station, the production crew told us that we wouldn't be needed for about two hours because they were running behind in taping the shows. This created another problem. If we stayed that long, we would miss our return flight, and I needed to be back in Poughkeepsie for classes the next morning.

I went into the bathroom to get some privacy so I could pray. Again, I asked Jesus to save the day. When I came out of the bathroom, the television crew said I would be on in five minutes.

As I walked into the studio, it dawned on me that I was not dressed for television—although, fortunately, I had shaved. One of the cameramen noticed my predicament and offered me his shirt and tie. We quickly changed, and before I knew it I was seated on stage and the introductory music was playing.

I had made it just in time, but there was one final problem: What on earth was I going to say?

As it turned out, I didn't need to have any prepared remarks. The show was called *Charisma*, and the host was Pat Robertson. For a half hour he asked me question after question. I was able to answer easily and gladly, sharing what I knew from my own experience of the great action of the Holy Spirit in the Catholic Church.

The show ended, I changed clothes again with the kind cameraman, and my traveling companion and I were whisked back to the Norfolk airport, barely making it on time. The plane landed in Baltimore before proceeding to New York. Then I realized another difficulty: We had taken off from La Guardia, but this plane was landing at Kennedy.

After we landed we ran out of the terminal, hailing a cab at the same time as a young couple. Simultaneously we said to the driver, "La Guardia." We all climbed into the taxi, so I figured that this was another opportunity to tell somebody about God's goodness.

I shared the story of my day with these people on the way to La Guardia.

I drove back to Marist College, dragged myself up to my dorm room and fell into bed at about 11 PM. As I reflected on my day, I realized that I had been gone for only eleven hours. In that time I had gone from Poughkeepsie to Mount Vernon, seen Harald, driven my car to La Guardia Airport, flown to Newport News and to Norfolk, taken a limousine to Portsmouth, shared about the Lord's goodness on television for half an hour, been driven back to Norfolk, flown to Baltimore and then on to Kennedy airport, taken a cab to La Guardia and then driven my car back to Poughkeepsie. And all I had said to start this adventure was, "Lord, I'm free this afternoon. If there is anything you want me to do, just let me know."

It is important to realize that this adventure began with a lot of uncertainty. After the fact, however, I was certain that the Lord had "spoken" to me. It's also important to note how subtle the initial experience was—the sound of a still, small voice that would have been easy to overlook, basically just a thought in my mind. I'm sure that if I had decided that the thought was not from God and had stayed on campus, Jesus would have loved me just as much. He would not have been angry with me at all. But what an adventure I would have missed!

HOW I HEAR THE LORD

The example I have just related is certainly not the only way I hear the Lord. I want to share now a list of ways I have "heard" God speak to me. The list is certainly not exhaustive. Some of the things I offer may overlap, but seeing them from different viewpoints can be helpful.

You may recognize some of these experiences. Hopefully they will help you realize some of the many ways God speaks to you. I trust that as you read, the Holy Spirit is going to be moving so that you will get more and more excited about hearing the Lord and, even more importantly, about *acting* on what he says to you.

Scripture, Tradition and the Church

I want to acknowledge the three most critical ways we should hear the Lord. These are Scripture, Sacred Tradition and the Magisterium, or teaching authority, of the Church. These three are not the main subject of this book. Although they are essential ways to hear the Lord, they are more than adequately dealt with in many other places.

Further, when we're asking, "What does the Lord want me to do *right now*?" we are usually not trying to figure out right from wrong. As I mentioned at the beginning of this chapter, we are trying to distinguish what are the good, better and best courses of action. Of all the things I *could* do, which one *should* I do in order to best serve God in the way he wants?

In these moments of decision, none of our possible choices should contradict Scripture, Tradition or the Church. Thus these teaching authorities are critical for discerning what we "hear" as answers to these questions. If one of my contemplated courses of action contradicts one of these three, then that course must be ruled out. Scripture, Tradition and the Magisterium, then, are both starting points for hearing God as well as good tests for discerning whether we are hearing God correctly by other means.

Anointed Teaching

The ability to teach spiritual truths is a significant ministry, both because it requires a gift from God and because he works powerfully through it. It's important to keep our ears open, because the topic the Lord is communicating about may not be directly related to what the speaker is dealing with. When we are in a situation that opens us up to God, he may nudge us with anything he chooses in the teaching: a word, a phrase, an implied topic.

That is what I experience when I'm listening to someone giving anointed teaching. "Oh, that opened up something for me. I really needed to hear that." Further, good anointed teaching, when it is opening up Scripture, Tradition and the Church, is a good tool for discerning whether a particular thought is from the Lord.

In an anointed teaching the Lord is using somebody else to speak to us. For example, this book is a teaching tool and hopefully an anointed one. I hope that as I share with you, the Holy Spirit will be touching your heart in a way that changes you. In fact, if he doesn't do this, then this work would be a colossal waste of time on my part. After all, you don't want David Mangan to try to change your heart—I'm not very good at it. That change is really God's job.

Practical Wisdom

Some people think practical wisdom, or common sense, is not really "hearing God," but I think it is. In Romans 12:2 Paul says, "Do not be conformed to this world but be transformed by the renewal of your mind." On occasion we behave as though that passage reads that we should be transformed by the *removal* of our minds.

Sometimes we don't want to use our analytical minds. We can act as though we are not allowed to think if we intend to be spiritual. We must realize that a *renewed* mind is a gift from God that we should really want to have. We want to *know* what God's will is.

Our minds are tools that God gives us for making good decisions.

People ask me occasionally, "I thought this, this and this, and I felt that way. Now, was that me, or was that God?" I usually answer, "Yes. It's you, *and* it's God, and it's supposed to be that way."

Don't try to separate these realities, because the Incarnation brought them together, and that is the way we are supposed to operate. Jesus became man and so made things that seemed natural supernatural, showing us that God loves to be entangled with us. Consider John 14:20: "In that day you will know that I am in my Father, and you in me, and I in you." What a wonderful heavenly mix-up!

Take Delight in the Lord

Psalm 37:4 says, "Take delight in the LORD, and he will give you the desires of your heart." One way to read a Scripture passage like this is that you should take delight in the Lord and then do anything you want. I don't think that's quite what is intended in this verse. I think the meaning is more like this: Take delight in the Lord, and he will change your heart so that your desires become more like his. That is, as you take delight in the Lord, he will put his desires in your heart.

These desires are another way in which the Lord will communicate with you. As you become more like him, the desires of your heart—although they may be yours—also have the hand of God in them. It's as though he plants a seed in you, and then the flower begins to come forth. That growth of the seed seems to be the most natural thing in the world.

You may get confused and think, "That just might be me." It might be you, but remember too that as you are taking delight in the Lord, he is changing your heart. Remember that the emphasis here is not on the desires of your heart but rather on taking your delight in the Lord.

This particular Scripture means a lot to me, because following its instruction changed my life completely. When I fell in love with my wife, I was delighting in the Lord, and after a while I came to realize that the desire I felt for Barbara came from him. I have this Scripture engraved in her wedding ring, reminding me that that is what she is to me.

Circumstances

God sometimes speaks to us through our circumstances. Unfortunately, this isn't always definitive. Suppose you're about to do something and a big obstacle comes up to prevent you from proceeding. That may be the Lord saying, "Stop, don't do that." However, he may be saying, "Push through it." Obviously, knowing which of these situations you're facing requires discernment, but the various circumstances in which we find ourselves can be great attention-getters from God, driving us to pray more. God is always present in our circumstances. The question is, how do we respond to them?

When Barbara and I were getting married, we wanted to buy a house, and we found one that we could afford. All seemed to be going well until the appraisal on the house was a little too low for the mortgage we were applying for. Our realtor assured us that this was unreasonable and could be easily remedied. This circumstance, however, caused us to stop and ask the Lord what he was saying in this situation.

As we prayed about it, we came to the conclusion that God had something else in mind for us. Even though we could have remedied the situation, we decided to tell the realtor that we thought the Lord didn't want us to proceed. We have never regretted that decision. The Lord moved us into other circumstances, which opened us to greater opportunities for his service.

Have you ever asked someone how he or she is doing and received the response, "Fine, under the circumstances"? A friend of mine used to answer that by asking, "What are you doing under there?" As Christians we are supposed to be *on top* of the circumstances, moving them the way God wants us to. And if we can learn to hear the Lord in the circumstances, we will be on top of them.

Spiritual Gifts

The Scriptures tell us in several places that God gives spiritual gifts to his people. In 1 Corinthians 12:8–11 we find a list of what are often called the charismatic gifts. In Ephesians 4:7–13 there is a list of what are sometimes called the ministry gifts. In Isaiah 11:2–3 we find the list of the "sevenfold gifts of the Holy Spirit" that we receive in the sacrament of confirmation. In Romans 12:6–8 we find yet another list of gifts. There are tons of spiritual gifts!

Sometimes God uses these gifts to communicate with us. I would encourage you to read these Scripture passages as well as others that you find that are related to spiritual gifts. The study of these gifts could be another book, but suffice it to say that spiritual gifts are meant for us today, not just for Christians in days gone by. God is still giving spiritual gifts to his people. Don't limit the ways in which the Holy Spirit wants to reach out to you.

We will consider this more in the next chapter.

Inspiration

By inspiration I mean general but strong "leadings" that are difficult to classify. Have you ever been wondering what to do in a situation and all of a sudden just known? Something happened inside of you, and you knew what to do. A friend of mine used to describe that by saying, "I just know it with my knower."

I had an important experience of "knowing with my knower" when I was a senior in high school making a college decision. I knew that my parents couldn't afford to send me across the street, let alone to college. This was just prior to when financial aid became need-based. The pressure was on: I needed to win an academic scholarship. I applied to two schools, the University of Pittsburgh and Duquesne University.

By early April I had received a full-tuition scholarship to Pitt, but I hadn't yet heard from Duquesne. I was invited to a dinner at a local service club to honor the top graduates from our school, and the speaker that night was the director of admissions from Duquesne. After the meal I went up to speak to him and to inquire about when I might hear about financial aid. He told me that the scholarship committee had begun meeting that day, and I had been awarded the first scholarship for full tuition.

I walked home on air, and for the next few days I played the role of the "sought-after senior." Each school had points in its favor. But Pitt had a good engineering school, and engineering was my intended major; Duquesne did not have a school of engineering at all. In addition, two of my brothers had gone to Pitt.

In the end I chose Duquesne. Why? Because I just "knew with my knower" that this was God's plan for my life.

I have never regretted that decision. It set me on a course that led me to even more of God's life. I didn't have any spiritual terms for what happened back then, but now I would call it inspiration: God was telling me something, and by his grace I responded.

Other People

Another way I hear the Lord is through people in my everyday life. I think he sneaks up on me this way sometimes. Perhaps somebody is saying something, and it hits me: God is speaking to me. Maybe the person isn't even talking to me, but the Lord seems to use what he or she is saying for my benefit.

Something else I've learned is that the Lord likes to speak to me through people I've had problems with or don't like very much. Thus, one of the things I've learned to do when I'm in a difficult relationship is to pray, "Lord, what is it I'm supposed to be hearing from this person that is from you?" Of course, this isn't always the case when I'm having a relationship problem, but I had better be open to that possibility. If the Lord can use me, he can use someone else too, including someone I don't like.

Christian Leaders

Another way we can hear the Lord is through Christian leadership. When the Lord raises up a leader in a given situation, he wants to use that leader. I don't mean to say that leaders are always right—not at all. However, leaders exercise a ministry that God has given to them. He may speak through them, so we need to be open to that possibility.

When I became the leader of a prayer group several years ago, at first I was afraid to give any direction to our meetings. I thought that I might "quench the Spirit" (1 Thessalonians 5:19). I didn't realize that God might actually want to use me to give direction. Believe me, before I understood this idea I presided over some pretty chaotic prayer meetings. Through these experiences I found that *not* exercising God-given leadership is often a quicker way to quench the Spirit.

Leaders are servants, and their job is to lead by following the Holy Spirit as much as they can. If the leader is actually hearing the Spirit and following him, then we might hear the Lord in what the leader is saying and doing. We must exercise discernment here, but if it's clear that God has placed someone in leadership in a particular situation, then the presumption is that we should be open to God's action through that person.

Being in Motion

Occasionally I'm in a situation where someone suggests that we take time to pray and listen to what the Lord is saying. However, that seems to be when I have the hardest time hearing the Lord. I find that if I'm in motion—if I'm doing what I need to do—I hear the Lord a lot better than I do when I'm sitting still. I'd be willing to bet that I have a lot of company in this.

We don't always need to stand around and wait for the Lord to speak before we can act. I like to say, "Do the next thing, whatever it is." As I do the next thing, I seem to hear the Lord a whole lot better.

When you're asking for clarity from God in a particular situation, you don't need to know everything before you do something. In fact, you probably already know a lot of things you should do. As you do the things that you can do, God will continue to direct you or change your direction. He might say, "Do this," or, "Don't do that," and then you can adjust.

An illustration may help to get the idea across. If you want to steer a car, it's a lot easier to do that while the car is moving. Even slight motion makes the car very easy to steer. I think that God is like that with us. He often wants us to be in motion when he does things so that he can direct us more easily.

Early in my teaching career, I had a sense that the Lord wanted me to teach in a different school than where I was at the time. I even had an idea of which school that was. I wasn't sure that this was God's leading, and I didn't even know if the other school was hiring.

One day after school I was praying about this decision. I decided I would visit the other school just to see what I thought. I figured that if it seemed like the place to be, I would go to the main office and request an application. This seemed like a reasonable idea.

As I drove to the school, I had an unusual sense that God was going to show me something. I wasn't sure about the sense, but I filed it in the back of my mind anyway.

I went to the school office, and I was asking for an application when the principal walked in. He overheard my request, invited me into his office and interviewed me on the spot. I had a job offer before I left! This never would have happened if I had just sat still wondering what to do.

There may be times when you have no idea what to do next, and stopping and waiting to hear the Lord is critical. Frequently, however, there is already something that you know you should be doing. If you do the job at hand, you may be surprised by what happens next.

Just Decide

In general I think that we ought to postpone important decisions until we can make good ones with God's wisdom. In the real world, however, things may be thrust upon us about which we must decide immediately. To make no decision becomes a decision in itself with important consequences.

In such times it is critical to remember that God does not ask us to do what we cannot do. He is not a God of frustration. If we must make a decision, then we must be capable of making one and making it well. God is with us in such situations, even though we may not be fully aware of it.

One area in life where this experience of feeling unprepared happens a lot is in raising children. Even though we try to have a unified plan as parents, kids have a way of thrusting decisions upon us for which we are seemingly unprepared. I have been amazed, time after time, at what God is able to handle if we give him the control.

I can be sure that God has equipped or will equip me to handle decisions and their effects. Even if I end up making a wrong decision, I can be sure that God will get me through to the right place. I'm not saying that I won't make a mistake; what I'm saying is that God can handle it if I do. And so, if I *must* make a decision, I make the best once I can and then start moving. I don't take that approach in frustration but rather with the knowledge that the Lord is somehow working in the situation.

Not Trying to Hear Him

I think that I actually hear God best when I'm not trying to hear him. When I have a big decision before me, I normally do the following: I gather the data. I pray about the issue. I think about it. I consider the details. I put it all in the "hopper" and let it mix around in my brain. And then I try to forget about it! I take a walk. I take a shower. I take a nap. I go out and play paddleball.

You would be surprised at how well this works. Often after I've done these things, all of a sudden I find that I know what to do— I just "know it with my knower."

Here's how I figure this works. On a physical level the human brain continues to process things even when we're not aware of it. This process also works on the spiritual level. All of the data is in there, and both our brains and our spirits are processing everything. We're not consciously aware of this continued development, but oftentimes we're hit with an inspiration, and it all becomes clear. "Aha! I know what to do."

Thus I find that getting away from a decision is sometimes the easiest way for me to hear the Lord. It's kind of an indirect way; I like to say, "He sneaks up on me." This method isn't foolproof, but I have found it to be very effective in a number of situations.

Getting a Scripture Passage
By "getting a Scripture passage," I mean this: You are considering a matter when a particular Scripture comes to mind. You look the passage up in your Bible, and amazingly it seems to address your very dilemma.

A variation on this is what I call "Bible roulette." People play this by closing their eyes, opening their Bible at random and letting their finger land on a page. Although I wouldn't recommend this method as the norm, I have seen it produce some great results. And why not? God does whatever he pleases, and sometimes he uses methods we would never expect.

A friend of mine was about to make an extremely important decision that involved a solemn promise, which in Scripture is sometimes called a "covenant." Although he felt fairly certain that God wanted him to make this promise, he decided to ask the Lord for a Scripture passage to confirm things. He opened what he thought was his Bible and put his finger on the page. When he looked down he realized that the book he was holding was a dictionary. Amazingly, his finger had fallen on the word *covenant*.

My friend had a good laugh. He also came to a deeper appreciation of God's love and mercy and care for him.

However, I think that most of the time asking for a passage is not the way to go. Although I have experienced the Lord's speaking to me in this way, I have also found myself pressing a little too hard on this button. One example of this happened when I was leading a retreat and things began to go wrong. In fact, they weren't actually going wrong; they only *appeared* to be going wrong.

The sponsors of the retreat had made a clear decision to not have any things happen that could be associated with the charismatic renewal. The "problem" was that charismatic things were happening, and I and the other leaders of the retreat couldn't stop them. During the closing sharing one young college student was so overcome by the Holy Spirit that he fell to the floor. Though he was obviously fine and enjoying a very peaceful experience, this was a little confusing to some people on the retreat.

Well, here we were at the end of the retreat, with various people standing up to share what God was doing with them, and this guy was lying on the floor. The situation was complicated by the fact that the person who had driven this young man to the retreat had been very explicit that there should be none of this "charismatic stuff" going on. Now this person was coming to the door to pick the young man up. I thought, "We're in trouble. The driver didn't like us when he dropped his friend off, and now his friend is on the floor."

The chaplain, the other leader and I stepped back from the scene to figure out what to do. One of us opened a Bible, put a finger on a page and found Proverbs 21:9: "It is better to live in a corner of the housetop / than in a house shared with a contentious woman." We stared at this passage for a moment and then started to laugh.

Imagine the scene: We already have a man on the floor while people are trying to share. Both those sharing and those listening must be wondering why their leaders are standing in the corner of the room laughing. Add to this the man trying to get in the door, whom other people are trying to stall so that he won't see the guy on the floor. Meanwhile we're getting this passage, "Better to live in a corner of the housetop than in a house shared with a contentious woman."

I quickly saw that "getting a passage" wasn't the way to proceed. Once I realized that we were barking up the wrong tree, a simple solution dawned on me. I walked over to the young man on the floor and said, "Why don't you get up? You're confusing some people." The young man got up, and everything was fine.

We had been over spiritualizing the situation, when all we needed was a little common sense. It's good that God helps us learn through our mistakes. I'm glad that I can look back and laugh at it now. Well, I even laughed then. It might have been stupid, but it was funny!

Spiritual Spillover

While the Lord is acting in a situation, we often can get understanding for something else entirely. I've had this happen to me many times. Perhaps I'm listening to someone speak or am reading something. I have a problem on my mind that has nothing to do with what I'm hearing or reading, but because the Holy Spirit is present and acting, I get the inspiration that I need.

I almost always carry a note card and a pen with me for just such occasions. I want to write down these inspirations right when they happen, because I know that I'll forget them otherwise. Be ready: You never know when God might want to communicate with you.

Dreams

I include this category because it occurs in Scripture, and several people have shared with me that the Lord speaks to them through dreams. One of the many examples in Scripture is in Matthew 1:20, where an angel of the Lord appears to Joseph in a dream to let him know that the Virgin Mary is with child by the Holy Spirit. Thus Joseph does not carry out his plan to divorce her quietly.

I don't think I have ever had the Lord speak to me in this way. I console myself with Joel 2:28, "Your *old* men shall dream dreams, / and your *young* men shall see visions" (emphasis added). Maybe I'm just not old enough yet.

In the Darnedest Places

The last way on my list of how we hear the Lord is a catchall. I can only say that he will speak in the "darnedest" places.

I once heard something in a movie that gave great direction for my life, and it wasn't a particularly holy movie. *The Princess Bride* is a comedy that makes fun of fairy tales and the movies based on them. The two main characters are Princess Buttercup and Westley. In one scene Buttercup orders Westley around and abuses him no end. She's quite obnoxious, but every time she tells him to do something, he merely says, "As you wish," and does whatever she demands.

As I was sitting in the movie theater, all I could think about was that one phrase. I started to pray, "Jesus, that is how I want to be to you. I want to be an 'as you wish' man." Ever since then, when I'm up against something difficult, I always try to stop and say, "As you wish, Lord."

More than twenty years have passed since I saw that movie for the first time, and "As you wish" is still my most common prayer. This is an old approach to spirituality that a modern movie reawakened the response in me. Let's be aware that God may inspire us at unusual times and in unlikely places.

A FEW FRIENDLY TIPS

We have now considered several ways of hearing the Lord. In no way is this meant to be an exhaustive list. If we were able to talk with each other, I'm sure that together we would find many more ways that God communicates with us. What I'm trying to do with this list is to awaken in you an eagerness to hear his voice, to listen for it at all times and in all circumstances. I also hope to stir in you recognition of what the Lord is already doing in your life and to broaden your horizons in considering how the Lord speaks to you.

In trying to hear God's voice, there are some things we should keep in mind. First, be careful of falling into the trap of expecting too much from one category. For example, you can't live your whole life by sudden inspiration. I tried it and found that I ended up sitting around doing a whole lot of nothing while I waited. You certainly want to be open to sudden inspiration, but you want to be balanced in seeking God's will, using other methods as well.

Have you ever seen the TV ad with the man who walks around with a cell phone asking, "Can you hear me now?" Sometimes I think that is what the Lord is saying to us: "Can you hear me now? Can you hear me now? Good."

God would really like us to hear him wherever we are all of the time. His direction can come right out of the Bible. It can come to us at Mass. It can come through another person. It can come through all of these things I've been talking about and more.

Remember that you already know what you need to do in most of the circumstances in your life. Someone once said that we know 80 percent of what we need to know, and I think that is a fair estimate. The other 20 percent is what can drive us crazy. That is when we ask, "Lord what do you want me to do now?" We need to remember that the Lord is there, and he wants us to know what to do.

Another thing to realize is that when the Lord does speak to us, chances are we won't fully understand right away what he has said. That's all right though! You'll find that your understanding unfolds as you go. You will tend to give the Lord's word an interpretation, and as it unfolds, you'll keep reinterpreting it. This is OK.

I once drove with three friends from Pittsburgh to New York to attend a conference at which another friend of ours was speaking. This happened during a time in our lives when we would jump in a car and drive seven or more hours to a conference because we didn't have many opportunities to attend them and we were very excited to see what God was doing.

On the way to New York we spent some time in prayer. As we prayed I thought I heard the Lord say to me, "You will have a chance to witness to many." I offered it to the others in the car as something the Lord may have said, so we would be ready for any opportunity that presented itself.

When we arrived at the hotel, I thought that maybe we should try to witness to a few people on the street before we went in, in response to what the Lord may have said to us in the car. However, we were late. We ran into the hotel looking for the ballroom where the meeting was being held.

As we entered the ballroom, we saw our friend up on the stage speaking to the leader of the meeting. The leader acknowledged the four of us and invited us to come up. We weren't expecting this; we merely wanted to hear our friend's talk.

We joined our friend on the stage, and the leader asked if we would be willing to share our testimonies with the whole group. There were about twelve hundred people in attendance at this meeting of the Full Gospel Business Men's Fellowship International. At that point my understanding of what the Lord had said changed from witnessing to a few people on the street to witnessing to twelve hundred people in the ballroom. This I never had expected.

I shared some of what the Lord had done in my life. The group seemed very interested in hearing about what God was doing in the Catholic Church, and I was glad to talk about that. Thinking that was the end of it, I sat down.

Then one of the sound technicians behind stage tugged at my shirt while the next person was sharing. "Oh, by the way," he said, "you were just broadcast over New York City radio." This again expanded the "many" the Lord had told me we would witness to. It now included an audience of more people than I could imagine.

I think that this often happens with God's word to us: Our understanding of what it entails keeps developing as we try to cooperate with his grace. Therefore, don't jump to conclusions, even when you think the meaning of a sense from the Lord seems obvious. Respond as well as you can, realizing that your under-standing has limitations—especially your knowledge of the future. As one wag has put it, "Very little is known of the unknown."

TRY IT!

Perhaps the most important bit of advice that I can give you in closing is this: Be willing to try, even if you make mistakes. I believe it was G.K. Chesterton who said that a thing worth doing is worth doing badly. This may seem a little strange compared with the way that adage normally goes, but I think it is helpful advice. If we wait until we can do something well, chances are good that we won't do it at all.

This business of trying to hear God is a learning process, which (almost certainly) involves mistakes. In most cases we only become sure that we heard the Lord after the fact. When we see the fruit that our acting upon his word bears, then we become certain.

I would like to encourage you to pray right now. Turn to God and ask him to help you recognize his voice when he speaks to you. Ask him for the grace to grow in this area of your life. Apply some of the things you have just learned.

Try to develop the habit of regularly asking God, "What are you doing right now? How can I help? I want to do whatever you want me to do." Listen for God's still, small voice. If a stray thought pops into your mind, it might be from God. I can't guarantee it, but you'd be surprised how often the Lord will do that.

If you don't get any great insight into what God is doing, remember that you already know a great deal. For example, when you walk into any room, one thing you know for certain is that God is actively loving everyone there. Ask yourself, "How can I join him in that love?" Do your best to respond to that call. I believe that this is the most sure-fire path to success in your life: Do what God is doing. You can't go wrong!

CHAPTER FIVE

Spiritual Gifts:
Ours for the Asking

IF WE WANT TO LIVE THE CHRISTIAN LIFE IN A POWERFUL WAY, WE must open up to allow the power of the Holy Spirit into our lives. One of the ways he gives us this power is through his spiritual gifts. This isn't just our good idea; it's God's idea.

We see in the directives of both the Church and Sacred Scripture that we should follow the impulses of the Holy Spirit and desire spiritual gifts. Saint Paul exhorts us in 1 Corinthians 4:20, "For the kingdom of God does not consist in talk but in power." And in 1 Corinthians 14:1 he says, "Make love your aim, and earnestly desire the spiritual gifts, especially that you may prophesy." And remember the plea of the Second Vatican Council to the laity, to give a "glad, generous, and prompt response…to the impulse of the Holy Spirit" (*Apostolicam Actuositatem*, 33).[1]

We need discernment as we ask for spiritual gifts, but clearly we ought to ask for them. I'll offer some approaches that can help us ask with openness and care.

THE REAL TREASURE

A good starting point is to consider what our central focus ought to be. As in all things in the Christian life, our focus is to be on Jesus. The things of God, important as they are, are never as valuable as God himself. All that we have and everything we do is for him, for his honor and glory.

In the early days of the charismatic renewal, many of us, me included, fell into the trap of wanting the gifts of God more than the Giver himself. As embarrassing as it is to admit, a lot of our attention used to be focused on spiritual gifts. Sometimes we would share which gifts we had experienced so far, almost as if we were keeping score.

On one level this makes sense. The experience of the more flashy gifts mentioned in the New Testament is very exciting, and being distracted by them is easy. Fortunately, Jesus is quite patient and rich in mercy.

One of the first times I experienced the gift of prophecy was when the Lord was gently correcting us. As we were praying, someone spoke a prophecy that consisted of only two words, "Praise Christ." When we heard that, we all knew that it referred to our focus being very wrong. We knew that we had to change. How ironic that the Lord used a spiritual gift to correct our imbalance in regard to spiritual gifts!

In God's wonderful kindness he showed us our errors and helped us to see that he is the real treasure. At the same time, he showed us the true value and function of all of his gifts, not only the flashy ones. All this is to say that we should desire spiritual gifts but in the right way.

I continue to emphasize desiring the gifts because it's more than OK to desire them; it's a good thing to desire them. I would go so far as to say that if we are not open to this desire, we are missing a part of what God wants to do for us. We also may be missing some of the tools we need for the job of serving him well. The spiritual gifts that God wants us to receive are not extras, not an added attraction. They are important for the job of advancing the kingdom.

DEEP AND WIDE

We need to be sure that our notion of spiritual gifts is broad enough. As we have already seen, there are several lists of gifts and references to specific gifts in the Scriptures. Let's look at some of them here.

Isaiah 11:2–3 lists what are often called the "sevenfold gifts of the Holy Spirit," which are emphasized in the sacrament of confirmation:

> And the Spirit of the LORD shall rest upon him,
>> the spirit of wisdom and of understanding,
>> the spirit of counsel and might,
>> the spirit of knowledge and the fear of the LORD.
> And his delight shall be in the fear of the LORD.

In 1 Corinthians 12:8–11 are listed what are commonly referred to as the "charismatic gifts":

> To one there is given through the Spirit the message of wisdom, to another the message of knowledge by means of the same Spirit, to another faith by the same Spirit, to another gifts of healing by that one Spirit, to another miraculous powers, to another prophecy, to another distinguishing between spirits, to another speaking in different kinds of tongues, and to still another the interpretation of tongues. All these are the work of one and the same Spirit, and he gives them to each one, just as he determines. (*NIV*)

Another group of gifts, which Saint Paul lists in Ephesians 4:11–13, are sometimes called the "ministry gifts":

> And his gifts were that some should be apostles, some prophets, some evangelists, some pastors and teachers, to equip the saints

for the work of ministry, for building up the body of Christ, until we all attain to the unity of the faith and of the knowledge of the Son of God, to mature manhood, to the measure of the stature of the fulness of Christ.

In Romans 12:6–8 there is yet another list:

We have different gifts, according to the grace given us. If a man's gift is prophesying, let him use it in proportion to his faith. If it is serving, let him serve; if it is teaching, let him teach; if it is encouraging, let him encourage; if it is contributing to the needs of others, let him give generously; if it is leadership, let him govern diligently; if it is showing mercy, let him do it cheerfully. (*NIV*)

These are not all of the possible references, but these serve to point out the broad spectrum of gifts the Spirit gives. There are flashy ones: prophecy, praying in tongues, healing. There are some we may not even have thought of as spiritual gifts: financial contributions, works of mercy, encouraging. The point is that these gifts span a lot of territory, and we should not operate in a narrow vein when it comes to the gifts God wants to impart to us.

We also don't want to exclude certain ways the Lord may want to act in our lives, even if some of these things have never happened to us before. I have met people who believe that there are certain ways the Lord deals with them and that's it. Although I gladly admit that due to our personality and disposition we may operate better in some arenas than others, I think we are missing something if we don't maintain the attitude that we want God to feel free to do anything he wishes with us, and by any means.

GET OPEN!

We need to be open to the surprises of the Holy Spirit. Being open to spiritual gifts and following the inspiration of the Holy Spirit, even when it comes in an unexpected form, has made a big difference for me and those around me.

I was recently in a meeting of national charismatic renewal leaders. As I looked across the room at one of those leaders, I felt that the Lord wanted me to go over to him, hug him and tell him that it was from Jesus. At first I was reluctant to do this. I was afraid that I would be embarrassed. After a little inner struggle I decided that the impulse was from the Lord and that I should do it. I went over to the man, hugged him and said that God wanted him to know that he loved him and that the hug was from Jesus.

The man broke down in tears. Just before I came over he had been feeling very low, like a failure to the Lord. He thought the Lord could no longer love him. When I hugged him, he genuinely experienced it as a hug from God, and it changed everything he was going through. His tears were tears of joy.

God gives gifts, but we need to receive them. People who are open to receiving gifts are more likely to use them. In this situation I was concerned about being embarrassed. Fear of embarrassment is one of many reasons that we may be slow to desire and ask for gifts.

Another reason that a lot of people are hesitant to open up to spiritual gifts is that they feel they're unworthy. If you feel this way, then you're very intelligent, because it's true. Who could be worthy of anything from God? But that is what makes a spiritual gift a gift: It is completely unmerited. We may be unworthy, but we are amazingly loved.

I think that one of the biggest deceptions that works against us today is the one that makes us think we are unlovable. We fall into the trap of thinking that God is just like us. We have to earn his love, and if we mess up, he has a hard time with us. But God is not like us! As the title of this book says, God loves you, and there's nothing you can do about it. You can't stop him.

If we want to receive anything from the Lord, the first step is always to accept his love. In Mark 10:21 we read of Jesus' response to the rich young man: "And Jesus looking upon him loved him." If you want those around you to accept God and his many gifts, first accept his love for you. Then help build an environment of love wherever you go.

ASK AND ACT

All this being said, how do you receive spiritual gifts? How can you spot them? Before I attempt answers to these questions, let me offer an encouraging thought.

It is very possible, and in fact it often occurs, that you can be using a spiritual gift and not be aware of it. Have you ever had someone tell you that something you said or did really helped, and you can't remember doing anything for that person? Or you remember it but it seemed like a natural thing to do? In those instances it's very likely that you were God's instrument for that person. You imparted a blessing from God with the spiritual gifts you already had, even if you didn't think you had them.

I have had people tell me that something I said in a presentation made all the difference for them. I've found myself thinking, "I wish I could remember what it was that I said so I could write it down and say it more often." Of course, it's not that those particular words are magic and produce some great effect. Rather, the Holy

Spirit was operating in the situation while I spoke, and he touched lives. I was simply a less-than-perfect servant trying to be obedient.

Now, how do we receive spiritual gifts?

Sometimes the deepest answers are the simplest. I would say: Ask and act. That is, ask God for what he has in mind, and be willing to act on what he says, or at least be willing to try. Matthew 7:11 says, "If you then, who are evil, know how to give good gifts to your children, how much more will your Father who is in heaven give good things to those who ask him!" The Father in heaven is more eager to give us his gifts than we are to receive them, so ask for them! Having asked, keep your spiritual eyes open. When a situation or opportunity presents itself, consider the possibility that Jesus may want to use you there. Sometimes the opportunities are obvious. Perhaps someone simply asks you to pray for him or her. Don't be afraid to do it there and then if it's appropriate.

PRAYER WORKS!

Not long ago I was sharing with a group of high school students. They took me at my word about God's wanting to bless us and asked if we could pray for some of them who wanted to be healed. I didn't feel particularly faith-filled, but I figured I needed to act on what I had said.

We prayed for one girl with a chronic stomachache, and her pain went away immediately. Another student wanted prayer for a painful wrist. Again, after we prayed the pain left immediately. A third student had injured her ankle and was supposed to get a cast put on the following day. When we prayed the pain left, and the following day her doctors said that a cast was no longer necessary. I don't think our faith was perfect; we were just willing to act.

Praying for healing may sound intimidating. My first thought when someone asks me to pray for healing is that I can't heal anyone—and that's absolutely true. However, I can pray, and my approach is simple.

I can always ask God for anything. I figure that he is interested in whatever the matter is because he is interested in me. I can't guarantee the results, but I can always do my part, and I can be sure that God will do his part. My part is to pray, and God's part is to love us however he chooses.

Amazingly, God often does heal the person I am praying for. When the prayer isn't answered in the way I want, then I have to trust. I can't do God's job, but I can do mine. I can pray and trust and I can encourage others to do the same.

Sometimes the impulses of the Holy Spirit can be very subtle, as was the "still small voice" of God mentioned in 1 Kings 19:12. Sometimes what appears to be a stray thought that doesn't seem to be from you pops into your head. At least consider the possibility that it may be from God. If after prayer and consideration you decide that it might be from him, act on it. You may not know any results right away. But then again, you may immediately be surprised to find that you're a part of something that the Lord is doing. In any event, you need to try.

One time I was praying with some of my high school students to receive more of God's love and power. One of the freshman girls was having a very powerful experience of God's presence and love. As I was encouraging her to serve God faithfully, I felt strongly that I should share something with her. I told her that there would be times of great difficulty and pain in our lives, and God is no less with us during those times than he is in the good times. When hard times come we need to rely on his grace, and he will see us through. What I had to say to her was common spiritual wisdom, but I felt with a sense of urgency that she needed to know it.

Our session ended, and we parted company at 9:30 that evening. About five hours later the principal of our school died in an auto accident. All of us were plunged into grief when we received the news as we returned to school in the morning. A few weeks later the young woman with whom I had prayed shared with me how important my words to her had been. She said they helped her navigate a time of great trouble.

Again, what I had shared with her was not an original insight. The power and comfort in the words came from the Holy Spirit, who was urging me to say what he knew she needed to hear at that time.

THE POWER OF GOOD COMPANY

One of the best ways to grow in the area of spiritual gifts is to associate with those who have experience in this area of the spiritual life. As we share with one another, we learn a lot, and we grow in new ways. We need the encouragement and support of others to grow in holiness and in any area of the Christian life, and this one is no different. This kind of support will help us discern God's will and help keep us from making serious mistakes.

We have to acknowledge from the beginning that we probably will make some mistakes as we try to grow in the use of spiritual gifts. It is fairly unreasonable to think that we will be able to learn anything new and be mistake-free while we are learning it. Our mistakes can be doorways to necessary growth. Brothers and sisters with experience can be a great aid to us in this regard.

This understanding of growing through our mistakes points out the great need for an environment of love. If you're in a situation where you know you are loved, you're much more willing to try new things, even if you might fail. You can trust those around you to pick you up and love you anyway. And you need to be prepared to offer that same love to your fellow learners.

It's also important to realize that, as with the baptism in the Holy Spirit, maturity isn't a prerequisite for receiving spiritual gifts. In addition, the gifts do not bring us to instant maturity, although they can be of valuable assistance in our growth. The high school students I referred to earlier have received and used spiritual gifts. They are still teenagers, however, and have a lot of growing to do. Their strength is that they look for guidance and help when they need it.

The mature people around us can help us grow in our ability to discern when things are from God and when they're not. Even when you feel as if nobody around you is very mature, the process of sharing with others is a great aid.

When you're trying to exercise some discernment for yourself or helping someone else along, there are a few simple principles and initial considerations that can help you get started. For one, our focus should be on discerning gifts, not judging people. The surest way to get people to shut down spiritually is to judge them harshly.

Think of it as gardening: A bush needs to grow a little wild before you can cut it back to a pleasing shape. If you trim the bush too early, you may stunt its growth or even damage it. People are very similar. We don't have to jump on every mistake or imperfection immediately; rather we should allow space and time for growth. Appreciate first the good things that the person does or tries to do. Only after we have shown this appreciation can we help others refine their understanding. In this way mistakes can be springboards to success.

When you are discerning or helping others discern, let love reign. You can allow for a little mess and still correct things. Major problems must be handled quickly, but in my experience, serious correction is not needed very often. Remember that God may give a gift to a person you don't like very much. That is your problem, not the person's.

KEEP IT SIMPLE

It is important to realize that spiritual gifts are ultimately not for the individual recipient but for the Church. God gives us gifts so that we may serve others more effectively. Simply put, we are the workers, and spiritual gifts are our tools for building up the body of Christ.

In all of these times of growth, never forget our primary resources: the Scriptures and the teaching of the Church. There is also a lot of good reading material on the subject of discernment, and the lives of the saints are especially helpful in this regard. They contain the wisdom of mature believers as well as stories that describe growth in maturity.

I have found that a good rule of thumb in discernment is that Christianity is simple. Be suspicious of anything that is overly complicated or secret. Consider 2 Corinthians 11:3: "But I am afraid that as the serpent deceived Eve by his cunning, your thoughts will be led astray from a sincere and pure devotion to Christ." The word translated "sincere" also carries the connotation of single-mindedness or simplicity.

But when I say that Christianity is simple, I don't mean that it's easy; I mean that it isn't complicated. Digging a ditch is simple in that it's not a set of complicated actions, but it is hard work.

There is one last thing to keep in mind when trying to figure out if something is from God. The things of God promote love, bring life, speak the truth and bear good fruit. The difficulty, however, is that we are usually not sure that something came from God until after we have responded. When we see what kind of fruit our actions have borne, then we see whether the word we acted on was from the Lord or not.

That's where faith and trust come in. If you're willing to try, you will learn, and you will get better at figuring out when you're hearing the voice of the Lord. Remember: Ask and act!

CHAPTER SIX

Now What?

YOU MAY RECALL THAT ONE OF THE QUESTIONS I ASKED IN MY account of the Duquesne weekend in the second chapter was, "What does God want of me?" I have been discovering the answer to that question day by day. Part of the answer is unique to me, but a large part of it is common to us all. We can ask together, "What should I do now as I live my faith in the power of the Holy Spirit?"

Many volumes have been written to answer that question. I will offer only brief advice here. Simply put, we must grow, serve and love. I'm going to share my thoughts about these areas in the order I have mentioned them, but remember that our attendance to each of them should be ongoing. As we grow we certainly will be able to love those around us in a better way. It is equally true that as we love those around us, we grow in significant ways. Service works into the mix in a similar fashion.

GROWTH

I once heard the question, "Why does someone who is called the Comforter spend so much time making us feel uncomfortable?" I have experienced a good bit of this discomfort in my life. Some of it is due to sin, and so its purpose is to bring us to repentance. However, part of the work of the Holy Spirit is to prod us to move forward. He makes us uncomfortable with where we are so that we will grow. I like to call this discomfort "a divine dissatisfaction."

This is one area of life where it pays to be greedy. No matter how much of the life of God I experience, I always want more. Fortunately he is eager to give us more. However, the "more" we will receive may not be comfortable.

Proverbs 4:23 says, "Keep your heart with all vigilance, / for from it flow the springs of life." The sense of the word *keep* here isn't to retain or to hoard; rather the word refers to keeping as in keeping a garden—that is, tending to it so that it will remain healthy and grow. Although growth in the Christian life springs from the grace of God, we need to take careful action to cooperate with that grace. Let us consider our "gardening tools."

Prayer

One of the primary tools is prayer. We need to maintain our relationship with the living God, and to do this we must spend time with him. At this point many of us will probably feel very inadequate. In fact, most people I know feel as if they don't pray very well. What I say to them is, "Do it anyway."

How do you expect to get better at something if you stop doing it? Recall Chesterton's statement: If a thing is worth doing, it is worth doing badly. He isn't encouraging us to accept poor performance; rather he is making the point that if we ever expect to do something well, we'll have to start somewhere. Therefore, don't evaluate your prayer; just do it!

When I mention prayer I'm certainly including participation at Mass and in all of the other sacraments. But don't limit prayer to those wonderful opportunities. We need to spend time alone with God and give him our attention as best we can.

How much time we spend isn't as important as our faithfulness in praying regularly. The length of time will vary with our circumstances. Keep in mind the image of caring for a garden. Spiritual growth takes time just as garden growth does. Be diligent, and be patient.

Scripture

Another key tool in our kit is Scripture. We need to continue learning about God and how to live a holy life. The Bible is the most significant book ever written, and it's ours for the taking. An old saying tells it all: "If you see a Bible that is falling apart, it probably belongs to someone who isn't."

The Bible is a gold mine, and we are the prospectors. Sometimes the meaning jumps off the page into our hearts, but sometimes we have to dig patiently and thoroughly. I would encourage you to read a portion of the Scriptures every day. Don't worry about how much; even a little will do. A good practice is to look up the readings for the Mass of the day.

In addition to the Bible, we have a wealth of great spiritual reading available to us, so much that it's difficult to make specific recommendations. I suggest you get the advice of those you trust about what to read. Also, reading the lives of the saints has inspired Christians for centuries. We can learn a lot from those who have gone before us.

Christian Community

We are not meant to stand alone; we were designed to live with others.

The word *community* is used a lot today. We are part of the world community; perhaps we are a part of the business community or another type of community. But whatever communities we belong to, in the first place we are members of a heavenly community—the Church. When we say that our citizenship is in heaven (see Philippians 3:20), this is more than a nice analogy. This is the environment that God has given to us for all aspects of our lives, not only our spiritual lives.

We need to avail ourselves, therefore, of the provisions that come with being a part of that community. For instance, the sacraments are not just a nice side option; they are tremendous opportunities for receiving infinite grace. Frequent the sacraments. Beat a path to the church door. You will find that this will buoy up your whole spiritual lives.

In addition to the sacraments, another gift in our community is the people who are in it. You tend to become like the people you hang out with, whether you like it or not. When you spend time with people who value what you value, you tend to grow in those values. To be sure, the Church is made up of sinners like you and me, but its essential nature is divine. We are God's people.

The quickest way that I know of to learn anything is by imitation. If you want to learn a skill, you find someone who does it well and do what he or she does. If you want to be holy, find some holy people and do what they do.

If we are wise we will not be minimalists in this regard, doing the least possible amount. The Church community is God's provision for us. Let's not dabble in it; let's live in it fully.

SERVICE

Just as we are not meant to be alone, we are not meant to keep what we have for ourselves. Any gifts we have received from God are not ultimately for us but to help us serve others. Not to serve others is like having a toolbox full of tools that you never use. Periodically you may pull them out and marvel at all of the wonderful things you have, but what a tragedy! These tools were given to you for a purpose: to serve.

Jesus made this purpose clear to us. Consider Matthew 20:26, 28: "Whoever would be great among you must be your servant…even as the Son of man came not to be served but to serve, and to give his life as a ransom for many."

A good question to ask is, "What service should I do?" The answer to this question will vary from person to person, but there are some things we all need to be engaged in.

A primary service that we all need to be a part of is believing in the Lord Jesus. Consider what Jesus says in the Gospel of John 6:28–29: "Then they said to him, 'What must we do, to be doing the works of God?' Jesus answered them, 'This is the work of God, that you believe in him whom he has sent.' "

Now, believing in the One God has sent doesn't usually come to mind when we think of doing the works of God. But let's not forget that believing is our most fundamental work. And out of the reality of believing we are called to be witnesses. Acts 1:8 says, "But you shall receive power when the Holy Spirit has come upon you; and you shall be my witnesses in Jerusalem and in all Judea and Samaria and to the end of the earth."

The normal outcome of receiving God's power is to witness to his glory. Often when we read Scriptures such as this one, we have a tendency to interpret them as referring to the foreign missions. However, note that the first place mentioned for the disciples to witness is Jerusalem—their own backyard. We don't have to go far to find a mission field. No matter where we go or what we do, there will always be people within easy reach who need to experience the goodness of God.

It is said that you may be the only Bible that some people will ever read. There may be many people in your life that will never be part of the Church or receive the sacraments or read the

Scriptures. Their only experience of what a holy life is may be through seeing you. Thus the most common witness we give, and perhaps the most important, is the way we live. In the words attributed to Saint Francis of Assisi, "Preach the gospel always. Use words when necessary." Of course we will fail at times, but even the way we handle our problems can be a witness to others.

We will find occasions when we need to witness with our words and at that time a holy life that people can see will make our words more believable. For many of us the thought of witnessing in this direct way is daunting. My advice is to keep it simple. A witness is merely one who testifies to what he or she knows to be true.

As far as what techniques to use or how forceful to be, keep in mind the following:

- If someone were witnessing to you, how would you want that person to act? Above all, you would want to be treated with respect. Most people don't like to be preached at.
- If your witness isn't being received very well, it is good to back out gracefully and with kindness. You want to leave the door open for someone else who may have an opportunity to share with that person at another time.

Even though witnessing is a service, when you share your faith with another person, you will receive more than you give. Educational research has found that the greatest indicator that material has been mastered is the ability to share it successfully with another. At the same time, teachers have discovered that when they teach something, they learn more about it. In fact, they have a saying, "You never know it until you've taught it." The same holds true for sharing your faith with another: When you do, your knowledge will increase, and your faith will be strengthened.

This is a wonderful heavenly paradox. The more you give your faith away, the more you receive.

We may not be experts in sharing the good news of Jesus Christ, but people are literally dying to know it. Even a poor attempt can yield infinite results. Give it a try!

THE POWER OF LOVE

You may remember that this final area, love, was the first area I addressed in this book. I was referring then to our experience of the love of God. Now I want to emphasize that this love is our fundamental gift to the world. We merely give away that which we have received. The love of God is both what we give and how we give it.

Like everything else in the Christian life, this task of loving is completely beyond our own resources. Yet Jesus can accomplish it in us and through us if we allow him. His grace is amazing! In Matthew 22:37–39 we read, "And [Jesus] said to him, 'You shall love the Lord your God with all your heart, and with all your soul, and with all your mind. This is the great and first commandment. And a second is like it, You shall love your neighbor as yourself.'"

Jesus is not in the habit of asking us to do things we cannot do. We can be certain that if he asks something of us, he will equip us to accomplish it, often beyond our wildest dreams. After all, this is how others will know that we are his disciples. "A new commandment I give to you," Jesus said, "that you love one another; even as I have loved you, that you also love one another. By this all men will know that you are my disciples, if you have love for one another" (John 13:34–35).

Love changes people, and expressing it has great power. When I met my wife's family, I found out right away that they were huggers. Any time I came into or was about to leave their home, I knew I was going to get hugged. This was new to me and very different from my experience of growing up. I knew that my parents loved me; they showed it in many ways. However, we were not a very demonstrative family when it came to expressions of love.

After meeting Barbara's family, I wondered if I could get my mother to be more expressive with her love. She was a wonderful woman, but I could not remember the last time she had hugged me or told me that she loved me. I decided to try a little experiment.

In my whole life I don't think I was ever able to change my mother's mind by using reasoned logic, no matter how compelling that logic might have been. Once she made up her mind, that was it—the matter was settled. I knew an argument wouldn't work, so I decided to do something very simple. Every time I would go to visit her (which was a few times a week), I would hug her and say, "I love you." I wasn't going to explain it; I was just going to do it and see what would happen.

The first hug was a little awkward, and when I said, "I love you," she responded awkwardly to that as well. However, in less than two weeks, things had changed completely. She seemed to look forward to my hugs on both arrival and departure. From that time forward she ended every conversation, whether in person or on the phone, with "David, you know I love you!"

SURE-FIRE SUCCESS

I would like to end by reminding you of my formula for success: Begin by trying to figure out what God is doing in whatever situation you find yourself. Next, ask God how you can best cooperate with what he is doing. Finally, cooperate with his action in the situation. You will then be a success by heaven's standards.

If you're unable to figure out what God is doing in your situation, remember that he is always loving everyone around you. Ask him what is the best way to love the people you're with, and then do that. Not only will you be a success, but you will be changing people's lives for the better.

May the Lord Jesus Christ be honored and glorified in all we are and in all we do!

Chapter Two: Spiritual Dynamite

1. Samuel Jacobs, quoted in Kilian McDonnell and George T. Montague, eds., *Fanning the Flame: What Does Baptism in the Holy Spirit Have to Do with Christian Initiation?* (Collegeville, Minn.: Liturgical, 1991), p. 7.

2. Walter M. Abbott, trans., *Documents of Vatican II* (New York: America, 1966), p. 521.

3. Leo Jozef Suenens, Foreword to Patti Gallagher Mansfield, *As by a New Pentecost: The Dramatic Beginning of the Catholic Charismatic Renewal* (Steubenville, Ohio: Franciscan University Press, 1992), p. ix.

4. Augustine, *Confessions*, Book 1, chap. 1, in John K. Ryan, trans., *The Confessions of St. Augustine* (New York: Image, 1960), p. 43.

Chapter Three: Walking in the Power of the Holy Spirit: Why Not You?

1. McDonnell and Montague, p. 7.

2. McDonnell and Montague, p. 7.

3. Raniero Cantalamessa, *Come, Creator Spirit: Meditations on the* Veni Creator, Denis and Marlene Barrett, trans. (Collegeville, Minn.: Liturgical, 2003), p. 54.

4. Cantalamessa, p. 55.

5. Cantalamessa, p. 54.

6. Homily of John Paul II, Celebration of First Vespers of Pentecost, Saturday, May 29, 2004, no. 3, www.vatican.va.

7. Pope John Paul II, Meeting With Ecclesial Movements and New Communities, May 30, 1998, no. 4, www.vatican.va.

8. Homily of His Holiness Benedict XVI, Prayer Vigil and Meeting, Solemnity of Pentecost, Meeting With the Ecclesial Movements and New Communities, June 3, 2006, www.vatican.va.

Chapter Five: Spiritual Gifts: Ours for the Asking

1. Abbott, p. 521.